disguised
Blessings

Jeanne Callahan Trantel

authorHOUSE®

AuthorHouse™
1663 Liberty Drive
Bloomington, IN 47403
www.authorhouse.com
Phone: 1-800-839-8640

First published by AuthorHouse 1/20/2010

ISBN: 978-1-4490-2837-4

Printed in the United States of America

For my sons, Stephen and Ryan, who taught me unconditional love

SPECIAL THANKS

I am deeply indebted to Jill Hofstra for her support in the creation of this book. Without her guidance, this publication would not have been possible.

FOREWORD

It is as if Jeanne Callahan Trantel was born to tell her story. When she speaks of the events that tore apart her marriage and her life, she does so with grace, poise, eloquence, and most of all, with honesty. Not an easy thing to do after it became headline news all over the New York metropolitan area that her life was not all that it appeared to be. Her husband, Stephen, had been living a secret life of his own. Stephen Trantel was no longer the Wall Street trader that Jeanne, his family, and his friends all thought him to be.

A tall, attractive redhead with a big smile, Jeanne is self-effacing and humble when she writes of the emotional and financial wreckage she has survived. She was left to pick up the pieces of a shattered marriage and manages to find her way to forgiveness and contentment. Her story is riveting. She is open and forthcoming about her struggles and triumphs, giving inspiration and hope for those facing financial and relationship crises in their own lives. – Jill Hofstra

ACKNOWLEDGEMENTS

There are so many people who have been such a blessing on this journey, and I would like to express my heartfelt gratitude.

I have so much gratitude and admiration for myparents, Bill and Patricia, who have gone beyond what is reasonable with their love, patience, and understanding.

To my boys, who have been my teachers of unconditional love, and who somehow walked into a maximum-security prison, filled with love and smiles.

To my two Brothers Richard and Paul for all their love and support. To my Callahan Cousins for all their support I love you all so much.

Many thanks to all my friends—Maria and Michael, Alison and Jeff, Kathy and John, Kerri and Terrance, Bried and Patrick, Brooke and Bobby, Wendy and Brian, Diedra, Missy and Pete, Beth and Brian, Martha and John, Jane, Chrissy G, Carla and Mark, Mary, MaryAnn and Kevin, Veronica, Alison and John, Lisa and Deb, Lynette, Lori, Helen, Maria, Mary Pat and Kevin, Maura and John, Jeanne F, Claudia, Elena, Angel, Jessica M, The Mawhinney kids, and Rita. And thanks so much to my friends and neighbors, Mary O'Shea and Pam Leake. I want to also thank Joe Whalen for his kindness, and Chris Fasano for his love and support. And special thanks to Joanne and Mike for all your support with the kids. Somuch appreciation to Vicki and Chris for always being there for us. And, to my dear friend Karen Hart, who sadly is now deceased.

Also, thanks to my support group on Wednesday nights. To Franz, my wonderful therapist, and my friend Jeanmarie for all our walks on the boardwalk and for never leaving my side. To Jen, thank you for all the nights in New York City and your fun-loving and caring friendship.

To my friend Ed Scannapieco, who continued to inspire me to write the book, and to my friends at Sky Athletic Club, especially Margi, Pam and Joanna, thanks for your kindness.

All my love and gratitude to so many of our family

members—to Mary Ellen and Rod for all your support and for the vacations to Wisconsin with the boys. To my cousin, Lisa, for being such an amazing person and for taking care of my boys and me when we needed itthe most. To Regina and Brenna, the Trantel family, Aunt Maureen and Uncle Moose, and Aunt Marie and Uncle Al—you have been so kind to me. I love you all so much.

Thank you to my Dayton, Ohio, girls and to my Chicago family; you were always there for me no matter what the distance was between us.

I am so appreciative of Mary, Pat and Tony for giving me my first opportunity in real estate.

Thank you to all of the Riverside School parents for their kindness. To Bruce at Accent On Eyes, to all my friends at Rave Cleaners, and to the community of Rockville Centre—thank you for your support.

Special thanks to the parish of St. Agnes for all your prayers and support.

And to my writer, Jill, for her patience, understanding, and dedication.

Because of all those people who were there for me in my darkest times, my life is rich and peaceful. It is now my turn to pass on these blessings to others. If my story can give strength and insight to just one other person, then I will feel that everything I have been through has been worth it. For each and every person who has touched my life in such a kind and positive way, I am ever so grateful! God bless.

CHAPTER ONE
JUST ABOUT PERFECT

"I love you."

"I love you too."

These were declarations Stephen and I made nearly every day, to each other and to our two little boys, Stephen Jr. and Ryan. As a fraternal twin, I was used to always someone by my side, even in the womb. I couldn't imagine ever being alone. With Stephen, my husband, I thought I had found the perfect mate. He took care of me and our children in ways that I was eternally grateful for. I never had worry with Stephen, not in any big way. We were a family.

I was living the American Dream. The stage was set and I thought I had the perfect life. I had always wanted a family and could not wait to be a mother. There I was. I had a loving husband and two beautiful, healthy sons. Everything seemed to be taken care of.

My biggest worries seemed to be what to make for dinner and teaching my two young boys the lessons that would hopefully make them great men.

After nine years of marriage, Stephen and I had finally been able to afford the perfect house for our family. We packed up our belongings from our starter home in Long Beach, New York, and moved into our dream home in idyllic Rockville Centre, New York. Although we were mourning the recent death of a beloved family member, Stephen's mother, we were hopeful about the future. It seemed as if things could only get better for us.

"We got the house!" Stephen said, smiling broadly.

"Really? I can't wait to tell the boys."

Rockville Centre is an affluent village on the south shore of Long Island, filled with pretty tree-lined blocks. The median income for a household in Rockville was over one hundred thousand dollars. I had grown up there and was eager to return, especially because of the prospect of living close to childhood friends and family.

Most of my childhood friends still lived in Rockville Centre and I looked forward to a life of barbecues and dinner parties. Many of my girlfriends had children around the same time I did and I was excited for our children to grow up together, going to the schools we had gone to, having play dates and birthday parties. I wanted my children to have the peaceful childhood that I had had in Rockville, sheltered from the harsher aspects of life. In Rockville, children could often be seen playing on the sidewalk. There are over 150 acres of parks and it is close to the beach. To me, it was home.

Our new house was a modest three-bedroom colonial on a beautiful street of medium sized houses with well-maintained front lawns. I was grateful to have a large backyard for the boys to play in and a large, airy kitchen to cook in. The house also had a garage, a large finished basement and a big attic. Stephen and I were both excited at the prospect of making renovations and really making the house suit our family's needs. We discussed pain colors and curtains. We wondered how the boys would adjust to having their own rooms. I could hardly believe my good fortune as I unpacked boxes of dishes and clothes. I placed each framed photo with care.

It was a relief not to have worry any longer about being landlords. Our starter home in Long Beach had been a split level and we'd rented out the lower half. After Ryan, our second child, was born, we knew that it was time to move. Although our house was a block away from the beach and we enjoyed going there frequently, two bedrooms was simply not big enough. We knew that the boys would eventually want their own rooms. Also, we were tired of sharing the space with the tenants downstairs. It was time for a bigger house, the house we would stay in until we grew old. The joy of having our own space without having to deal with tenants below outweighed the stress of a bigger mortgage payment. Besides, Stephen assured me that we could afford it. We both wanted the best for our children and this house, in Rockville Centre, where we'd always wanted to settle, was the best. The boys ran from room to room, shouting and laughing. I was looking forward to hearing that sound for a long time.

Poverty was not something one saw much of in Rockville. Nor did one see a lot of crime. Only thirty-five minutes from New York City, many of its residents, like my husband Stephen, worked on Wall Street. Because of its proximity to the businesses of Manhattan and the ease with which one could take the Long Island Railroad into the city, it was a popular place to live amongst affluent businessmen and their families. For us, it was the perfect setting to raise a family. Although Rockville Centre is a community close to the energy, opportunities, and excitement of Manhattan, it still has a small-town, friendly feel, and almost everyone knows his or her neighbors.

Stephen grew up in Nassau County, Long Island, only a few towns away. We both had active lives with a lot of our family and friends surrounding us. My father, an attorney, lived in Rockville, and Stephen's father, a retired NYPD police officer, lived there as well.

Our backgrounds were similar, as were the values we had been brought up with. Stephen and I looked forward to passing down those values to our sons. We had both been raised Catholic and were fairly traditional. I had a happy childhood; Stephen told me that he had a happy childhood as well. My family had been slightly more well-to-do than his, but neither of us had ever wanted for anything. Both of our mothers were very involved in the raising of the children and both of our fathers were hard-working and successful. Both of us remained close to our families, speaking with family members several times a week. Since we both had loved living on Long Island as children, we were thrilled to return as adults with children of our own. Our dream had become a reality.

I grew up in an upper middle class home with attentive parents who made sure I was well taken care of. My parents owned the house we lived in and we had two cars. We were able to go on family vacations every year. I never had to think or worry about money in a serious way. My mother, a children's librarian, took several years off from work to be home, only going back to work when my brothers and I started school. I grew up waterskiing, playing tennis, and hiking in the woods with my family.

I was always Daddy's little girl, the only girl among three children. My brothers protected me as well. All of my friends loved coming over to my house. Sometimes my father would take me and a group of my friends to Coney Island for the day where we would get on the rides and eat hot dogs. I remember laughing a lot as a child. My twin brother Richard and I were very close and spent a lot of time together. I don't remember ever feeling lonely.

Although I never wanted for anything, my parents were careful not to spoil us children. My father made sure that we understood how privileged we were. He pushed for me and my brothers to learn the value of a dollar by working. Although I never thought much about money, I did like the independence that having money gave me. I enjoyed not having to ask my parents for money when I wanted to go to the movies or buy a pair of shoes. I liked being able to afford gas for my car. In high school, I worked at a greeting card store. I remember standing at the register, flipping through Get Well cards and Birthday cards for hours. To this day, I still remember some of the sayings in those cards. I also delivered papers and worked at a bagel shop. At the bagel shop, I managed to put on several pounds because of all the bagels I consumed. It didn't bother me, though. It was satisfying to get an actual paycheck.

My mother took me to the bank so that I could open my own bank account. Because I made my own money, I was never particularly frivolous. Like many teenage girls, I enjoyed shopping at the mall, browsing through clothing stores and music stores, but I was always aware of wanting to save.

Having my *own* money was important to me and my parents encouraged this independent streak in me. Yet, even though I was independent, I was not particularly rebellious. I was not perfect, and I certainly made mistakes, but for the most part I was a good Catholic girl. I didn't defy my parents and they never had to worry about me getting into serious trouble. I had one steady serious boyfriend throughout high school and never felt the urge to recklessly experiment with drinking or drugs.

After high school, I went to Johnson and Whales College in Rhode Island. This was the first time I had been away from my family and the first year was difficult. In college, it was assumed that I would work to help out with expenses, although my parents paid my tuition. During college I worked as an elevator operator in Learner's clothing store. I also worked at a topless bar as a waitress, pulling in a lot of money from tips. It never occurred to me to try to make more money by being a dancer at the bar. I couldn't imagine taking my top off for a room of strangers and then letting these strangers place money in my underwear. I just wasn't that sort of girl.

By the time I received my Associate's Degree, I had so much money saved from waitressing that I was able to pay my own way when I went to Europe with some girlfriends. This made me and my parents proud. I majored in Travel Tourism and was eager to travel to other countries. I had always wanted to see the world. While in college, I had another serious boyfriend, but by the time of graduation we had drifted apart.

I traveled around Europe, catching another glimpse of life outside the little world of Rockville Centre where I had grown up. Although Rhode Island was a distance away from Long Island, it was quiet, safe and somehow felt familiar to me. The streets of Amsterdam and to other European cities like Paris and London were unlike any I had seen before. They were overflowing with constant excitement. The pulse of those cities was fast, and I loved their cosmopolitan feel and being exposed to such different cultures. Growing up in the suburbs of New York City, I had always thought I was worldly. I started to realize on my trips to Europe that my Long Island life had kept me quite sheltered in many ways. For the first time I really noticed how little some people had compared to me and realized how lucky I was.

When I returned home from my jaunt around Europe, I was thrilled to land a job with American Airlines in their ground passenger service department at nearby JFK Airport. I readily took advantage of the company benefits and the ability the job offered for me to travel. I was twenty-four years old, single, and had the freedom to enjoy doing all the things young people do. It was fantastic, and I loved it. It was exciting to be in the travel industry, to be around so many people all the time, to enjoy the people I was working with, and to be employed in a position that was as far as I could possibly get from a regular office job. Around this time, I went back to school for my Bachelor's Degree.

At the same time, as much as I enjoyed touring and being exposed to the different places my job took me, I was still always happy to come back to my hometown. At heart, I was still a daddy's girl and I never liked being away from my family for too long. I lived at home with my parents when not travelling, and I was quite content to be within the confines of where I grew up, especially because I was surrounded by the people I had known all my life. As I look back now, my world was small, safe, and very secure. I spoke with my twin brother Richard nearly every day.

Eventually I decided to rent a beachfront house with several girlfriends. We thought it would be fun to live on the beach, hanging out on the sand whenever we weren't at work. We were right. Every day felt a little bit like a party. I worked, went to school and laughed a lot with my friends. Being able to lay out on the sand whenever I wanted to and to feel the ocean between my toes was delicious. I was young, fun-loving and hard-working. I was also searching for something, although I didn't know for what at the time.

Around the time I moved out of the house, my parents calmly announced that they were separating. This was one of the biggest shocks of my life and it took a long time for me to recover from it. I had thought that my parents would be together forever. I don't remember them fighting much when we were growing up. Both my mother and my father were generally good-natured people, a quality that all of their children possessed. My mother didn't shout; my father didn't yell. I couldn't believe that they could just fall out of love and break up the family that they had spent a lifetime to create. My parents assured me and my brothers that we were still a family, but I couldn't help but feel anger and sadness. No longer would my parents live together; I would have to visit them both separately. The house where I had grown up and had so many happy memories of would be forever changed. I remember praying. It felt so wrong; our family was Catholic and although we weren't particularly devout, the divorce of my parents seemed to go against everything that we had been raised to believe. I always thought that when you married someone, you stayed married to them no matter what. The idealism of my childhood was damaged and an insecurity settled somewhere deep inside of me.

I met Stephen Trantel in 1991. One evening, my girlfriends and I planned to meet at a bar in Long Beach for dinner. I arrived first. As I was waiting for my friends to get there, I caught the eye of the handsome young man working behind the bar. He was full of energy, confident, and quick to smile. He was also very efficient, working hard to keep everything behind the bar clean and orderly while also serving drinks. His movements were conservative, yet energetic, like those of a lion.

"I'm Steve."

"Jeanne." I giggled nervously as he looked at me. His smile was wide and inviting.

The bar wasn't very busy yet, so we had time to talk for awhile before my friends showed up. I don't remember what we said, although I suspect it was the usual things people say upon first meeting. I do remember thinking that he was unlike many young men in their twenties, at least the ones that I knew.

Stephen seemed to really have his act together. He was ambitious and hard working. He told me that he was a clerk on the trading floor of Wall Street by day and a bartender by night. He seemed to know exactly what he wanted out of life. Success, and lots of it. I admired the self-confidence he possessed, especially since I wasn't as confident about what I wanted. My parents were in the middle of their divorce and everything felt uncertain. I was in school, but I wasn't quite sure what the next step would be for me.

I felt an instant attraction to him, to his ambition and focus and ready smile. By the time my girlfriends arrived at the bar for dinner, I had come to realize he was someone I could see myself spending a lot of time with.

Over the course of the night, Stephen, being a skilled and witty bartender, was friendly with everyone and gave a lot of attention to each of the patrons. He was charming, outgoing, and by all accounts, a very popular person. He could charm anybody. At the end of the night, he asked me for my number as I was leaving with my two girlfriends. I was taken by surprise.

"Hey Jeanne, wait a minute. Can I call you sometime?" he asked.

"Sure," I responded, fumbling around in my purse for a pen and a slip of paper. He handed me a napkin and a pen. I scribbled my name and number on the napkin, my hand shaking a little. My two girlfriends looked on with great interest, smiling and nudging each other. As we left the restaurant, I was filled with both the food I had consumed and hope.

I hadn't thought he was very interested in me. He talked with everyone, so there had been no reason for me to feel special. I stole glances at him from the table I shared with my friends, only half listening to what was being said to me. Needless to say, I was more than happy to give him my phone number. After giving him my number I immediately wondered when he would call, or *if* he would call. *What if he didn't call?* The thought was humiliating.

He called me the next day, his voice sounding smooth and relaxed on the phone.

A few days later, I again went to the bar where Stephen worked, this time just *pretending* to be meeting my girlfriends. Stephen and I had been talking on the phone. I wanted a chance to see him again. That night, as we talked at the bar, there was no doubt in my mind that there was chemistry between us. Before I knew it, we were doing more than simply talking at the bar or on the telephone. We were friends for three months and then we were dating. My relationship with Stephen was unlike any of my previous relationships. We were serious, almost from the very beginning. He made me feel special in a way that none of my previous boyfriends had.

Almost immediately, the tone of our relationship was set. Stephen liked to take care of me and I grew used to being taken care of by him. He liked to pay for everything; he wouldn't allow me reach for my wallet. Stephen had come from a traditional Italian family in which the man always takes care of things. He opened doors and walked on the part of the sidewalk closest to the street. He liked to "be the man". Flowers, jewelry, fur coats, dinners – he loved showing me how much he cared for me by giving me things. I remember receiving entire outfits from him – dresses, shoes, stockings. I was like his little doll and he loved dressing me up.

Stephen was stability in a world that had become unstable with my parents' divorce. He encouraged me to finish school and pursue a career, although he made it clear very early on that he wanted a woman willing to stay home with the children, should children come. His mother was a traditional Italian mother who doted on him and his siblings. She made meatballs and lasagna from scratch. On this point, I agreed. I wanted a family and I wanted to be there for my family. After my parents divorce, I wanted this more than ever.

Like all couples, we had our arguments. Mostly these arguments had to do with Stephen's desire to control. My general attitude was always more laid-back than his. For example, a messy closet and dishes in the sink didn't bother me. Stephen couldn't stand for things to be out of place. He was a great labeler, marking things in his freezer and cupboards. He hated inefficiency – lateness, messiness, laziness.

Although Stephen liked to "be the man" I didn't always appreciate "being the woman". He could be exasperating in his need for perfection. However, we were in love. Talking things out and making up never took very long.

After one particular fight, knowing I wouldn't be home, Stephen went over to the apartment I had just moved into. He left me a large plant that he had bought for my living room. I remember arriving home and running my fingers along the leaves. Later that same year, on Christmas day, he told me he had a big surprise for me. I couldn't imagine what it was, though I wondered if it might be a puppy. He took me to his apartment, opened the door to his bedroom, and led me in. A fur coat that he had bought for me was draped over his bed.

"Do you like it?" he asked anxiously, like a little boy. I did. Lavish gifts were a constant part of my courtship and I admit that I loved them, although I loved the man giving them to me more. He was sweet and funny and kind and the nicest man I had ever dated. I felt taken care of and safe with Stephen.

I suppose the most pivotal point in our relationship happened on one of our dates, though it wasn't the date itself that was memorable—it was what I felt inside that night. I remember meeting him at the Rainbow Room in New York City. The Rainbow Room was an upscale restaurant and bar on the sixty-fifth floor of Rockefeller Center. After cocktails and dinner customers could dance the night away on the dance floor. Seeing Stephen that night, I thought, *This is the man I'm going to marry*. I was wearing a short black dress, and he was already seated in a booth, handsomely dressed in a suit, waiting for me to arrive. The maître de walked me to the table, and as I was on my way over to him, time seemed to slow down to a near stop. I had a feeling I had never before in my life had. The love I felt for Stephen in that moment was so deep. The certainty of knowing I would spend my life with him was as close to an out-of-body body experience as I had ever had. I simply *knew* I would marry him.

Two years later, that is exactly what we did.

CHAPTER TWO
SOUL MATES

The weekend Stephen proposed we spent in New Hampshire. I knew that the proposal was coming because he had been hinting at it for months. I was ready. He picked me up from work and I remember noticing that he had gotten monogrammed floor mats for his car that said "Stephen" and "Jeanne". He actually got down on one knee when he asked me and I didn't think twice about saying yes. Being traditional, Stephen even asked my father for permission. My parents had an instant affection for Stephen. They were just as seduced as I was by his easy charm and confidence. The night they met him, my mother invited Stephen and me, along with my father, over for dinner. It was nice to see my parents together, even if just as friends. At dinner, Stephen spoke passionately about his future plans. My father was impressed with his focus and drive to succeed. My mother thought he was very sweet.

"He seems like a good guy," my father said, a little grudgingly.

"I like him," my mother said. Both of my brothers liked him as well. He seemed to fit right in, talking with my father about business and with my brothers about sports.

My meeting of Stephen's parents went just as easily. I met them at a family function along with Stephen's siblings and some of his extended family. His family was loud and warm and wonderful.

We were engaged for a year and I remember that year being one of happy planning for the wedding with my mother. We poured over bridal magazines together. I tried not to think about how my parents' marriage had ended. I knew that Stephen and I were meant to be together and that we would stay together forever.

"This is the dress," I said when I tried on the dress I knew I would get married in.

"You look beautiful," my mother said, tearing up.

I looked forward to going to bed with Stephen every night and waking up with him every morning. Because we both came from traditional families, we chose not to live together before we were married.

The anticipation grew greater as the date became closer.

After we got engaged, Stephen's thoughtfulness and generosity continued. I was able to plan our wedding and focus on the details of what would become one of the best days of my life without worrying about money. My parents insisted on paying for the wedding. I was twenty-seven years old when I got married. Everyone in my still tight-knit family loved Stephen, including my grandparents. This was a relief as I don't believe I *could* have married someone that my family didn't approve of.

Stephen and I were married at the Bar Association in Garden City. My father walked me down the aisle and proudly gave me away, looking very handsome in a dark suit. I floated towards my future husband as if in a dream, no doubt in my mind that I was doing the right thing. We had our wedding ceremony at a large church in Rockville Centre with close to two hundred people in attendance.

Stephen seemed like he might cry when he saw me walking towards him. I could think else but him and our life together.

"I, Jeanne, take you, Stephen, to be my lawfully wedded husband. To have and to hold, to honor and to cherish, from this day forward..." The words slipped from my mouth easily.

The wedding celebration had all the makings of a traditional, classic, elegant wedding, from the band to the flowers and the delicious food. I loved my wedding dress; it was long, straight, and sleek with exquisite beading. I felt like a queen in it. I still remember the taste of my wedding cake and the rich, delicate texture of the frosting. Our friends and family were as thrilled as we were; there was a unanimous feeling that Stephen and I belonged together. The wedding was the happily ever after that I had dreamed of as a little girl and Stephen was my Prince Charming.

After our fairy tale wedding, we spent nine incredible days on our honeymoon in Antigua's Jumby Bay, a small little island in the Caribbean. Since I was still working for the airlines, we were able to get amazing discounts, making the trip that much more enjoyable. I don't remember ever being in a place, before or after, more luxurious than Antigua's Jumby Bay. Antigua's Jumby Bay was a popular vacation spot for very wealthy people and celebrities. While on our honeymoon, Stephen and I were surrounded by the luxury of wealth and we enjoyed every moment of it. We were off to the perfect start.

For the first year of our marriage, Stephen and I lived in a beachfront apartment.

"Let's go to the beach," I said often. It was wonderful to have the beach at our doorstep and we spent many romantic evenings walking along the sand and planning our future. Stephen told me that he thought I looked beautiful whether I was in a swimsuit or a bathrobe. Living together proved to be natural and easy for both of us. I often couldn't wait to get home from work so that I could spend the evening with my new perfect husband, talking while preparing and eating dinner. We both worked full time. After we got married, Stephen wasn't as enthusiastic about me working. He had visions of a wife who stayed at home as his mother had, taking care of the children and making elaborate Italian meals. I wanted to please him and was eager to start a family as well, but I still worked out of necessity.

After our first year of marriage, Stephen's parents helped us in buying our first home in Long Beach. It was modest, but ours. We enjoyed the process of decorating it together. It was a duplex and we were able to rent out a part of it to help with the mortgage.

I would describe our marriage as idyllic in the beginning. Stephen and I had many common interests.

We were best friends and we were very much in love. We were a fun-loving couple who truly enjoyed each other's company and doing things together like skiing, biking, and traveling. We loved taking walks together, going camping, playing cards at night, and taking our truck out to Robert Moses Beach where we would spend hours upon hours fishing and talking.

Stephen talked a lot about money; how to get it, keep it, save it, spend it. He was driven by a deep desire to succeed. I supposed it was because it was the way he was raised. His father was strict and had ruled the children with an iron-discipline. Stephen had always worked, even as a young boy. I didn't understand his obsession with money, although I liked having nice things. To me, money was always about the things you could get with it. I didn't care about being rich, I simply wanted to be comfortable. I didn't want to have to *worry* about money.

We started our married life in Long Beach, the town where we both met, only a few miles from Rockville Centre where we would eventually buy our dream home. We enjoyed living close to the beach and spent a good deal of time with both of our families. We had a large but close-knit circle of friends and socialized with many couples that we had both known since childhood. Stephen's friends became my friends and my friends became his. We lived a simple and modest, but comfortable life. Stephen was making more than enough money to support the both of us, although I still worked; one year he made around $300,000. My job provided us with health benefits which we both agreed was a necessity. Stephen was trading on his own at that point, so we didn't have insurance coverage through his job.

At that point, more than my job, my focus was on creating a beautiful home and family for us. Stephen's mother was an amazing cook so I focused on learning how to cook meals that Stephen would enjoy. She was also an amazing housekeeper, so I worked to make our home clean and inviting. Stephen also made it clear that he didn't necessarily want me to have a job.

"I want to be the breadwinner. You can stay home and take care of the children."

"We don't have any children."

"Not yet. But we will."

After two years of marriage, we were blessed with our first son, Stephen. I continued to work part-time after Stephen Jr. was born, receiving help from Stephen's mother who would often babysit. The birth of my first child was life-changing for me. Suddenly, I was profoundly responsible for another person.

"Look at him," I said to Stephen, staring at our son. "Just look at him." I was in awe of this little person that Stephen and I had created and I wanted nothing but the best for my child. Having a newborn can be challenging on a relationship, but Stephen and I managed to push through the sleepless nights with good humor. Stephen and I managed to stay connected with things like date nights.

Four years later, we had our second son, Ryan. We were both thrilled. Stephen was making good money in Manhattan on the commodities floor. He provided a comfortable lifestyle for our family. We lived in a nice home and in a nice neighborhood. After the boys were born it still wasn't necessary for me to have a full-time job and Stephen never wanted to have the boys in daycare.

"Why send them to daycare when we have my mother to help out?" he would argue. "You should just stop working."

When our second son, Ryan, was born I stopped working. We both agreed that I would be the traditional stay-at-home mom and not have to try to balance the children, the house, and a career.

I was thankful to have that freedom and threw myself into making a happy and healthy lifestyle for us all. I had many other friends who were also at home during the day with their children. It seemed that we all had children around the same time. In addition to shopping, cooking, and cleaning, I was busy with play dates and providing plenty of activities for the kids. I really loved the outdoors, especially the beach, and so I would often take the boys in a double stroller and walk the boardwalk. We were always doing *something*, and I enjoyed every minute of it.

Motherhood suited me well, and Stephen loved being a father. He never hesitated to jump in to help care for the boys, and they absolutely adored him. As a hands-on father, Stephen never shied away from changing diapers, getting up in the night with the children, or doing the things that many times are typically left for the mothers to do.

Stephen also paid all the bills, not wanting me to have to deal with our finances.

"I'll take care of it," he'd always say and I got used to letting him take care of it all. It never occurred to me that I should be more involved. After we got married, we had a joint bank account. When I stopped working, it seemed natural that Stephen would take care of the finances. He had two accounts, a work account and a family account. When he needed to he transferred money from the work account into the family account. Stephen was the breadwinner; I was the homemaker. We were both comfortable with this arrangement and I didn't feel the need to challenge Stephen's manhood by insisting on knowing how we spent every cent. In a sense, money felt like a man's arena to me, like sports and business.

When I stopped working to stay home with the children, I noticed Stephen's desire for control increase slightly, but it didn't bother me much. For example, he began handing me a menu at the beginning of the week, mapping out all of the family meals. Every morning I made lunch for Stephen to take with him to the city and I liked doing this for him. There was a strict schedule for dinner and if we were off schedule, it would bother him. He labeled everything, from food to clothing, and was uptight about laundry. Because I was in the world of babies, a world of diapers and spit up and food on the floor, I didn't really understand his uptight attitude. However, even though I was always a little more easy-going than him, I indulged his regimented, very particular tastes. Toothpaste lids, meaning the lids actually being placed neatly on the toothpaste tube, were an issue for him; toothpaste lids were never an issue for me.

After Ryan was born, Stephen and I always made sure that we still had our time together as a couple. We did our best to keep up a tradition of going out for a "date" once a week, and we often stayed up late talking or playing cards. Our relationship was strong; we were totally committed to one another, and we were both very much devoted to our family. Though we made sure we spent the weekends doing activities with children, kept up the tradition of doing Sunday night dinners with Stephen's family, and got together often with friends who had kids the same age as our children, our relationship as a couple always remained a top priority. He really was the love of my life and I believe that I was his.

The other top priority for Stephen was his job; I had always known that his career was important to him in a way that a career was never important to me. Although trading was an extremely high-pressure profession, the market was good. In the beginning, Stephen seemed to thrive in the fast-paced environment.

"It's the best job when making money and the worst job when losing money," he would say. He used to tell people that going to work was like being in a football game every day. Some days you'd win, some you'd lose, and there were always a lot of other players on the field.

There was lots of action every day, and he loved the challenge of Wall Street.

Though it was certainly exciting at times, it was also a constant roller coaster. Stephen's job on the trading floor was extremely stressful with lots of highs and just as many downs. He was gambling with his money – our money – every day without knowing where a trade would leave him financially at the end of the day. He was fully aware of the big risk he was taking and regularly felt the pressure of that responsibility, especially after the birth of Ryan. He wasn't one to hide how he felt. Over time, I grew accustomed to his mood swings. On a good day, he was in a great mood.

"I won at the market today!" he would exclaim, giving me a big squeeze.

On bad days, when he lost a lot of money, his mood showed it. He was like the weather, both predictable and unpredictable. I never knew when a storm would come, but I got used to expecting storms.

Anyone married to a Wall Street trader knows what this is like; one week we had a lot of money, the next it was gone. You just get used to it after a while because you have to. The stress about needing to still somehow keep a budget to ensure financial security for the family never quite diminishes, but it's easy to also believe that it will all somehow work itself out.

I was not involved in planning the family budget; this was my way of alleviating the stress of never knowing when we were going to have money or not. Also, this was how Stephen wanted it. Stephen was very controlling, especially when it came to money. Although he was generous with money, providing me with everything I needed, he liked to be the one to give it away. He never wanted to talk about bills and debt with me. In fact, he seemed annoyed whenever I questioned our ability to afford something. Because of Stephen's confidence, or arrogance, I never became too worried about our financial situation. I just assumed that everything would be as it always had been; we would always have money, or a way of getting money. I had never been in a situation in which I didn't have money, even as a little girl. Although I was not a frivolous person and knew the value of a dollar, somehow being married to Stephen had lulled me into a feeling of comfort. I just didn't worry about it. I wanted to believe that Stephen had it all under control. I had faith in him, just as I had had faith in my father when I was a little girl. I was confident that the man in my life would always make sure that I was safe and taken care of.

Every month Stephen handed me a wad of cash, usually $1,000, to pay for groceries and things like that. There was never a month when he didn't hand me money.

Despite the dangers of trading, Stephen and I were satisfied with his job and the success he often had. Like most of our neighbors, many of whom also worked in Manhattan, we were living a comfortable life. For the most part, our life was simple and relatively worry-free; we had no big problems to speak of.

Outside of work, Stephen had an active life. He had many friends he liked to spend time with, and at home, he was adept at doing repairs and odd jobs. "What can I fix?" he'd ask. I always considered Stephen to be the opposite of lazy. He was handy around the house and constantly doing something. Though he wasn't a plumber, if there was a leak somewhere in the house, he knew how to fix it. He did a lot of the construction work that needed to be done in the house, too, including putting in new windows. If he couldn't figure something out by himself, he asked a friend to help him or show him how to do it. The job always got done. He was the type of person who, after doing all our lawn work and trimming the hedges, would wander over and help the neighbors by trimming their hedges as well.

Though we didn't take nearly as many vacations after the children were born, we still made full use of our weekends and time off. We were no longer using our time share and going to the Bahamas, skiing in Vermont and New Hampshire, or spending the sporadic night in New York City—as we had before the children were born—but our "at home" vacation time was always special for us. Stephen made it a point to spend lots of time with the boys and me, going to parks, camping, and lounging on the beach. As often as we could, we would take the boys biking and hiking. We were always busy, and always together as a family.

Then came September 11, 2001 and the World Trade Center disaster.

CHAPTER THREE
Loss

That morning Stephen missed the train into the city. I had been in a car accident and the car was in the shop. He had to take a cab to the Long Island Railroad which made him late. Had he been on time, he might have been at the World Trade Center, where many of his friends and colleagues were. He walked past the World Trade Center every day on his way to work. It was lucky and frightening and devastating all at once. He might have died. That day I remember being glued to the news and holding my children close. I remember screaming. I also remember desperately attempting to reach Stephen who was stuck on a stalled train underneath Penn Station for hours in the midst of all the chaos.

Twelve hours went by before I could reach Stephen. Within that time I took Stephen Jr. to preschool and nursed Ryan who was five months old. It was a great relief to finally hear Stephen's voice and know that he was safe. I knew how blessed we were – we had our families and each other, all that mattered.

Nearly three thousand people died because of 9/11. Long Island was filled with communities where many people lost a great deal. Places like Long Beach and Rockville Center were hit hard. It seemed as though everyone was in mourning. In the weeks following the tragedy, many of our neighbors buried or memorialized their loved ones. Stephen and I went to at least five funerals. It was heartbreaking. Everyone knew somebody who died, or somebody who had lost a loved one. Several of Stephen's business friends and associates had died during the attacks on the World Trade Center. There was a certain degree of guilt in surviving.

Suddenly the United States was at war. We were invading Afghanistan and we were launching a War on Terrorism. Like the rest of the United States, I was shaken. My safe little life no longer felt safe. However, to deal with this feeling of insecurity, I buried myself deeper into my family. I clung to my children and to my husband.

Financially, Stephen and those Wall Street associates of his who did survive, lost a lot of money on 9/11. The commodities floor windows had been blown in. The floor closed for two weeks. This meant that Stephen lost two weeks' worth of money.

This was the beginning of a change in our marriage. Stephen became moodier and less open with his feelings. Feelings of guilt, trauma and anxiety began to get in the way. Stephen and I had started to move away from each other, although I didn't realize it at the time.

We were so focused on the tragic deaths that surrounded us that neither Stephen nor I realized how the ramifications of 9/11 would eventually affect our financial position and, ultimately, our future. As Americans, we were all affected emotionally, but Stephen and many others like him were also deeply affected professionally. That day caused him to lose two weeks' worth of work and thousands of dollars. Following 9/11, Stephen went back to work, but eventually lost his job.

After six months of searching for a new position, he was still down on his luck. He had started to dabble in real estate in Rockville Centre and actually got his real estate license, but he never made one sale. No matter what money-making scheme he tried, nothing seemed to work. Finally, Stephen decided to return to work as a trader. This time, however, he worked on his own. He traded crude oil with his own money. Stephen rented a seat on the COMEX Exchange, spending 9:30 AM to 2:30 PM in the "ring." I did not realize it at the time, but an individual trader with limited funds and high expenses was in a very tough position. I was very concerned, however, when he returned to trade because I knew he was not the great trader he had once been; somewhere down the line, he had lost his touch.

"Why don't you get a real job with a steady paycheck?" I suggested gently. I encouraged him to go in that direction and was constantly his cheerleader, but in the end, you can only cheer for so long; he had made his decision and was determined to stick with it.

"I'm just gonna stick it out. Things will get better," he said. I don't know that Stephen could see himself as anything other than a trader. He seemed to think that if he could not be successful at this one thing, especially since had experienced success in the past, he was a failure.

The pressure was intense, and in many ways, Stephen, now trading on his own, seemed even more anxious than when he had been out of work. He had always been a smoker, but now he constantly had a cigarette in his hand. This time around, his work as a trader started to take a heavy toll on our family life and marriage. It wasn't as easy to go along with the predictable roller coaster I had grown accustomed to. The roller coaster had become extremely unpredictable. To make matters worse, whether things were up or down, Stephen was *always* high-strung and anxious. At times, he would snap at me and the boys over trivial things.

"Pick that up! This place is a mess!" he would yell at the boys.

Eventually, this type of behavior became the norm instead of the exception.

It was clear to me that he was not a happy man. I started to grow very concerned about the state of our marriage and suggested that we get help. He agreed to go to counseling with me to work on our relationship. For a short time, it did help. I remember laying on the floor of the therapist's room, attempting to communicate our feelings. However, in retrospect, seeing the therapist was only a small Band-Aid for a much bigger problem. Eventually, Stephen refused to go.

I remained extremely concerned about his behavior and was worried about what the stress he was experiencing could potentially do to him. Without a doubt, he was not living a healthy lifestyle. He stopped working out even though he had always taken great care of his body.

"Why don't you go the gym and work out? It might relax you," I'd say.

"I'm not in the mood," he'd respond. He stopped eating well and lost weight. He stopped seeming to care about anything except making money and more of it.

Making matters even more stressful for him, when we moved to our dream house in Rockville Centre, we took on a sizable mortgage—double the amount of our previous mortgage. It was one of the peaks in the real estate market, though we wouldn't realize that until later. Buying the house seemed like the right thing to do at the time, as we had definitely outgrown our old house and we were able to sell at a high market rate. We also bought our new house at a premium price. Stephen was confident that we could afford it, and I trusted his judgment. We loved our new home and it gave us a great deal of satisfaction and pride to know that we were raising our two sons in a community with an outstanding educational system.

"Can you believe this? We finally made it," I said to him.

I had no idea that during that time—when we made the move and bought the new house—Stephen was having a great deal of trouble trading. He owed hundreds of thousands of dollars on the floor to his clearinghouse. He kept me in the dark about it and assured me we could afford our dream home in Rockville Centre. At the time of the move, Stephen had been trading on his own for two years, so it wasn't new to him, but as I came to find out later, his trading just kept getting worse and worse. The more financial pressure he was under—because of the huge sums of money he was out—the more he seemed to lose his edge.

After our move to Rockville Centre, I had some early concerns about Stephen. He was not the easy going man I had married, and he had started to become excessively moody and more irritable. I knew that many people, like Stephen, who worked downtown, were having a hard time coping with both the emotional and financial fallout from 9/11. It was extremely difficult for everyone in the country, but being down there every day and having to walk by ground zero was horribly depressing. He had walked through the Twin Towers every day to work and had lost a lot of friends. Like a lot of other traders, Stephen lost a lot of money on 9/11. That's when our money troubles really began, although I was ignorant about that. I attributed his moods to the overall depressing climate at the time. I just kept telling myself that Stephen was going through a phase, and I believed that eventually he would return to being himself.

Unfortunately, things took a dramatic turn for the worse. During this tumultuous financial crisis, the reality of which Stephen was keeping to himself, his mother became terminally ill with a rare brain disease. It was a terribly debilitating illness. Suddenly Stephen's mother who had always been vibrant and strong was weak and in pain. No amount of money could make her better. It was extremely difficult to deal with the hopelessness of her situation. I was very close to her also and had spent a great deal of time with her before she died.

When she died it was a great loss to our whole family. She had played a significant role in our lives, constantly spending time with our two boys, helping with the children whenever we needed it, cooking and inviting us over for Sunday dinners, and being there for Stephen whenever he needed someone to talk to. In many ways, she was the center of the family. The impact of her death was devastating for the entire family, but particularly Stephen. After her death in September 2002, Stephen expressed that he was angry with God, something he would never have said before.

Between the market and the illness and death of Stephen's mother, the roller coaster we had already been on only increased in speed and severity. Stephen was a high-energy person, and though he was not afraid of a challenge, it was an extremely difficult time for him both personally and professionally. During this entire period, he could never sit still—not for a second. He always had to be doing something—anything. He would find odds and ends to fix around the house, even when there were none that needed attention. And when he couldn't find anything else that "needed" fixing, he would spend time in the shed doing woodworking, one of his favorite hobbies.

"Are you coming to bed?" I'd ask him.

"In a little while, I'm just gonna finish this." His head was bent towards his work, away from me. When he came to bed, I felt a growing distance between us.

Although Stephen hid the real facts of our financial situation, I sensed how much stress he was under and saw how much anxiety he was exhibiting. I suggested I get a job to relieve some of his pressure. I truly had no problem with working except for my reluctance to leave the boys; I had always worked, even though it had been a few years since I'd had a full time job. I was more than willing to help us get back on our feet.

Stephen, as always, insisted I didn't need to work, that everything was fine, and that we would have no trouble affording our new home in Rockville Centre because of the money we had made when selling our previous home. He said he wanted me at home with the children and that he didn't want me trying to juggle a career and motherhood. I didn't push the matter. Perhaps I should have. Frankly, I loved being at home with the children. I didn't want to miss any part of their growing up.

All things considered, I still felt very lucky, and it seemed that—together—we had a whole world and a whole life in front of us. The difficult times would pass; of that I was sure because they always had in the past. I was confident that Stephen would eventually get through the manic, highly stressful phase he was in; it was just a matter of time.

Each day, I packed Stephen's lunch as he headed to the Long Island Railroad for the commute to his job on Wall Street. I stayed at home, committed to fulfilling my role as a supportive wife and devoted mother. I felt that we, as a family, even through the rough and trying times, were content and had much to be grateful for. We had each other and that was enough for me. We moved into the house in Rockville Centre in the spring of 2003. Although Stephen was still very depressed over his mother's death, I hoped that the move would be a fresh start. Signing the deed on closing day was a moment of great pride for me. The boys loved their new rooms and Stephen seemed to relax for a short while as we unpacked and settled into our dream home. Friends and family helped us get settled and I wasted little time in setting up play dates with friends who had children.

Stephen continued to have a difficult time dealing with his mother's death. He religiously attended a prayer group for awhile, but eventually stopped going. The following year showed a Stephen's gradual withdrawal from me and the boys. He was a changed man, no longer the enthusiastic, driven man that I had known. He began to spend more and more time in the basement, away from me and the boys.

Something in him died when his mother died. He became more irritable, snapping at me over the littlest details. He lost more weight. He looked older and pale. I didn't know how to help him, especially since he refused to talk about what was bothering him. I knew that he and his mother had been extremely close; she was a good woman and yet she had been allowed to suffer and die by God. Stephen refused to accept this.

That winter I noticed that Stephen seemed to falter

professionally, but as usual he refused to discuss it seriously whenever I brought it up. I busied myself with the Stephen Jr. and Ryan, delighting in watching them grow. I didn't know how to reach Stephen and hoped that eventually, in time, he would return to his old self, the funny, charming, optimistic man I fell in love with. I pushed my sense of foreboding aside and tried to ignore all of the signs that something was very wrong with my husband.

CHAPTER FOUR
Unraveling

We went on vacation in July 2003.

"Are you sure we should go?" I asked since I suspected that we were doing worse than Stephen was letting on.

"Don't be ridiculous, of course we're going," he replied. We had a wonderful trip to Wisconsin and visited with childhood friends of mine for two weeks. My grandparents once had a summer cottage there on a beautiful, tranquil lake in the Northwoods, and it was a place I visited each summer when I was growing up. It's a place that brings you to peace and helps you let go of all your problems, at least for the moment.

While there, Stephen didn't seem to be able to get comfortable "in his own skin." I thought there was something very wrong with not being able to relax and "let go" in this serene environment surrounded by all the beauties of nature.

"What's wrong with you?" I asked him.

"Nothing's wrong," he insisted.

On the trip Stephen paid for everything in cash. I remember noticing with surprise at one point that he was carrying a large wad of cash.

I said, "Wow, you must be doing great at work!"

He nodded in silent agreement but he didn't smile.

I met him outside the Commodities Exchange one Friday afternoon after our return from our vacation. It was my birthday. Stephen and I spent the night in Manhattan and had dinner at a very nice restaurant in the city to celebrate. It was almost like the old days, before his mother's death, the house mortgage and other bills that seemed to be tearing us apart. The next day, we stayed in the city.

"Let's go shopping," Stephen said.

"Are you sure?"

"Yeah, let's just go. I want to take you shopping. It's your birthday."

I was a little uncomfortable with how much money we were spending, but Stephen assured me that it was fine. I remember stopping a drugstore with him and being amazed at the fervor with which Stephen grabbed random items to buy.

"Steve, come on! What are you doing?" I protested. It was ridiculous, all of the things he was stocking up on. He seemed to want to get rid of all the money in his hands.

One day in late summer of 2003, while my mother was at work, there was a huge commotion and someone yelled that the bank next door had just been robbed. She was horrified and called to tell me about it.

"Can something like that happen in Long Island in broad daylight?" I asked. We were both amazed. It was a frightening thing.

It was early September 2003. My girlfriend and I were having "girls' night out" and going camping.

"Let's take Steve's truck," I said to her.

"Are you sure it's okay?"

"Of course it is." I usually didn't drive Stephen's truck. It was larger than my SUV and better for carrying all our camping gear. Stephen really did not want me to take it and complained as he took a large duffle bag and cleaned out the interior for me.

"I don't feel like cleaning it. You should just take your car," he said. He spent a long time and kept going back into the truck, rearranging things and stuffing more and more things into the bag. I thought it was odd that he was spending so much time cleaning out his truck and that he was so irritated with me. I couldn't understand why he didn't want me to drive the truck.

Another night I was very upset when we got into bed. Stephen had been angry and short with me for several days. It had become normal for him to tell me to "shut up". I hadn't been able to communicate with him, and he just could not settle down. He was refusing to eat or even talk.

I asked him, "What's wrong with you? If it's your job doing this to you, get out of it! I could work."

Stephen cut me off quickly. "No, no, I don't want you to work; that's not an option. You need to just leave me alone."

He turned his back to me and had nothing more to say. I know he must have heard me cry myself to sleep that night, but there was no further conversation.

It was Halloween, October 2003. I went to a costume store to pick out outfits for a Halloween party we were attending. I quickly picked out jailbird costumes. The costumes were like those worn by characters in old comedies—big and baggy with thick stripes. Something had drawn me to those outfits in the Halloween store; they were my first and only selection. As we got ready for the party that evening, Stephen came out of the bathroom fully disguised with a mustache and a dark, dark wig. He looked so creepy all dressed up like that. It was fear I felt when I looked at him; it was not at all humorous or fun. I knew something was very wrong, but I didn't know what.

It was November 2003. Montauk is at the very east end of Long Island and had always been one of our favorite places to go to as a couple and as a family. We took the boys there for a weekend. It's a very peaceful, relaxing place, so if someone is stressed out there, it really stands out. Stephen couldn't seem to relax.

On the first night, when we returned to the motel after taking the boys for pizza, Stephen parked the truck with the back end toward the door of our motel. I thought that was a little odd, but I didn't ask him about it. Stephen was a little strange that night and he was unusually quiet. I sensed worry. I felt he wanted to talk and to have some time alone with me, but the boys were still awake. Eventually I think we all fell asleep at around the same time. Whatever he wanted to say remained unsaid that night. I wish that it hadn't.

Another evening Stephen and I were watching a local news story about a bank robbery in Rockville

Centre. The man was eventually caught later on. At the time, we were both taken back by the news report.

"Can you believe that? Bank robberies in Rockville Centre? How crazy is that?" I asked. It was surprising enough that we had heard of robberies taking place on Long Island, but right in our own town! Stephen agreed with me that it was quite scary.

Later that fall I told Stephen that I thought I had a stalker. I had noticed a car parked outside our house, and it seemed like it had followed me a few times when I left the house.

"What should we do? Why would somebody be stalking me?"

Stephen just blew it off. He told me that the idea of a stalker was ridiculous.

"You're just imagining things," he said. "Who would stalk you?"

I was uneasy but shrugged it off because Stephen had made me feel silly about the whole thing.

It was the day before Thanksgiving 2003. Stephen and I had made plans to the boys into New York City for an overnight trip. Stephen booked a hotel in Manhattan so that we could watch the balloons being inflated for the Macy's Thanksgiving Day Parade, have dinner, stay overnight, and then be there early enough to get a good spot to view the parade on Thanksgiving morning. We had looked forward to this event for a long time, and we were happy that the boys were finally old enough to enjoy it. At this point, our sons were three and seven.

Although Stephen usually left for Manhattan each day by 8:30 AM and was home by 5:00 PM, he had the occasional luxury of working by phone or from home, and he could direct his buy and sell orders through his clerk. That morning was one such day when he did not commute. Stephen did, however, spend the early part of the day at the real estate office in town where he had recently earned his sales license and was working part-time as an agent (though he wasn't making any sales).

Several months earlier, Stephen told me he was feeling the pressure and volatility of Wall Street and wanted to become licensed as a real estate agent in order to expand his career options. Stephen also had looked into purchasing a donut machine to sell to restaurants and entertainment venues, and investigated other ventures that could be a second career when he was ready to give up the stressful profession of Wall Street trading. I understood and supported his new endeavors. I truly believed the job to be the source of most of Stephen's stress.

I knew that the market was tough and it showed on him.

"It's just money!" I'd say in an attempt to lighten the mood. "Who cares?" I didn't understand why he was so stressed about money. There were more important things in my mind, like our relationship and the health of Stephen Jr. and Ryan.

"Easy for you to say. It's not just money," he'd respond. Even though he didn't want me to work, he seemed to want me to feel guilty for all of the work that *he* was doing. I didn't know what to do.

When he was at home, he was almost manic. He was no longer just keeping himself busy every moment of every day. One minute he would delve into household projects, tearing apart closets, cleaning the garage, and the next minute he would be lethargic or napping, almost in a depressed state. He was eating even less, had lost a lot of weight, and frequently had insomnia. I would wake up in the middle of the night to find him watching TV.

"What are you watching? Come to bed," I'd say.

"I can't sleep," he'd respond.

In the weeks leading up to Thanksgiving, Stephen had been particularly restless.

I had definitely started to feel the strain in our relationship, but I really didn't know what to do to fix it. I didn't know what I was doing, or not doing, to contribute to how bad things were getting between Stephen and me. I tried to get him to talk to me about work and the pressure he was obviously feeling, but he refused. He was flying off the handle with me and the boys more and more often now.

On a rare occasion out with our friends, Stephen was noticeably jumpy and snapped at everything I said. Our friends noticed; it was impossible not to. I confided in one of my friends that night, and then later to my mother, that I was worried about our marriage. I knew it was in trouble.

"I think we're in trouble," I said to my mother. "What should I do?"

"Talk to him," she said.

"He won't talk to me. I can't make him." I privately wondered if he might be having an affair. I wondered if he was still feeling the effect of his mother's passing. I just couldn't understand why my husband, my best friend, the man I thought I knew better than anyone, had changed into someone I didn't recognize.

Given the explosive current of the previous months, I was looking forward to our night away in the city and then spending the rest of Thanksgiving weekend as a family.

A few days away from work will do him good, I thought.

On the day we were heading into the city, I went into town and spent the morning walking around with my younger son, Ryan, shopping and running errands. We stopped by the real estate office to visit Stephen that morning—just to say hello and find out what time he wanted to leave for the city later that day. Stephen was at his desk, which was by the front window, reading the newspaper. As soon as we walked into the office, he snapped the newspaper shut. I had no clue why he was so agitated and short with me.

"You should be home packing for our trip. Why are you wasting time here? I want to head into the city early today and you have a lot to do," he practically yelled at me.

That was not the kind of greeting I had expected.

"Go home right now and finish packing! I'll be there and ready to leave in an hour," he snapped.

I was worried because he seemed so distracted, and it looked like something was very wrong with him. Nevertheless, I went home with no argument and packed the car as he had asked me to. I didn't want Ryan to see us fighting.

As I mulled over his strange behavior in my mind

while packing up, I faced up to the fact that he had been acting that way for some time now. There had been an obvious strain between us for awhile. He rarely spoke to me anymore. He kept to himself and stayed up much later than me every night. We never had fun together anymore. After moving to the new house we had stopped having date night which had always been an important opportunity for us to reconnect with each other. Now I always felt like I was walking on eggshells when I was around him. Even in our own home, I felt uncomfortable and nervous. We used to laugh together all the time and genuinely enjoy each other's company; our friends always used to say that we had such a good marriage and that we were such a great couple. I agreed with them; we *did* have a good marriage and we *were* a great couple. I missed those times. As I finished getting everything ready for the overnight trip, it became more and more clear to me how big the wall between me and Stephen had become.

Though the way he treated me when Ryan and I stopped in to say hello had really upset me, I tried not to show it. As usual, I chalked it up to the stress of Wall Street and his job. *Every marriage goes through difficult times*, I thought, *and maybe this is ours.*

I was uncomfortable with the way things were

between us, but I resolved to put his moodiness and outbursts aside, at least for the holiday weekend. I felt I owed it to the Stephen Jr. and Ryan.

When he came home a short time later, the car was packed as promised and we were ready to go, but he was visibly upset and seemed to be in complete panic mode. Ignoring his mood, I got the boys in the car, and we got going. On the way into the city that afternoon, Stephen drove like an absolute lunatic. His anxiety level was the highest I had ever seen. I was starting to get more and more irritated with him, instead of simply worried. He weaved in and out of traffic, driving way over the speed limit and darting between cars. Our three-year old, Ryan, was in his car seat in the back.

He yelled up to Stephen, "Slow down, Daddy!" The boys were as frightened as I was becoming.

I reprimanded Stephen for driving so fast with the boys in the car, and an argument soon followed.

"C'mon, Stephen! Slow down! What's going on with you? Why are you driving like such a mad man?" I asked.

Stephen retorted with, "I have to beat the traffic!"

That was the last thing he said on our way into the city. He never slowed down and ignored me for the rest of the ride. I spent the rest of the ride with my focus on the backseat, interacting with and talking with the boys.

Stephen was on his cell phone a lot during that afternoon and evening. Although I did not hear the conversations, I assumed they were work related and was annoyed because in the past he had always made it a point not to bring his work home with him. I could not understand what could be so pressing with work on the eve of Thanksgiving and a holiday weekend. We had one of the biggest fights of our marriage that night in the hotel after the children had gone to bed.

"What's going on with you? Tell me!" I yelled.

"Just leave me alone!" he yelled back. It ended when both of us were too tired to fight anymore. All of my questions remained unanswered.

I tried to keep the rest of the trip as pleasant as possible. I held on to hope that this getaway might still somehow be able to restore the wreck our marriage had become. Mostly, I was tired of confrontations and arguments. I just wanted things to go back to the way they had been before, when we lived our simple life in Long Beach. I wondered if moving to Rockville Centre had been a mistake, although I loved the house. Ever since we had moved, Stephen had become more and more difficult. It was beginning to affect the children.

A lot of planning had gone into this special getaway in the city with the boys, and I was determined not to let it be ruined by Stephen's moods. I'll never forget the look on the boys' faces as they watched the balloons being blown up in preparation for the Macy's Thanksgiving Day Parade.

"Look Mom!" Ryan gasped, giggling. The excitement was palpable and contagious. The boys watched the "backstage scene" with the kind of wonder that they did at Christmas when they came down the stairs with their eyes wide. I felt that excitement, too, and even Stephen was enjoying the boys and their reaction. For a short window of time, Stephen seemed to calm down and genuinely enjoy himself.

That night, with the boys in tow, we met friends at a gourmet deli in the city for dinner. They had two boys the same ages as ours, so I was sure it would be a fun night out for everyone. We all sat at one big table, with Stephen sitting at the end. Shortly into dinner, Stephen's moodiness and jumpiness returned. He was restless and kept getting up from the table to make a phone call or go outside and smoke while pacing back and forth. He seemed unusually nervous, had no appetite, and was snapping at everyone—especially me. I could tell my friends thought he was acting very strange.

"Steve is making us a little uncomfortable," one of our friends eventually admitted. "What's with him?"

I knew he was even more stressed than usual, and while I tried to be understanding and supportive, I was embarrassed to have to justify his behavior for our friends. I was more and more angry with him.

"Sorry," I apologized through gritted teeth. I made excuses to our friends for his behavior, knowing that he was completely out of control and not knowing why.

After dinner, when we returned to the hotel, Stephen and I exchanged angry words, though not in front of the boys.

"You're embarrassing me and yourself! Why can't you put your phone down for dinner? How rude are you? You owe me an apology!" I yelled.

"I don't owe you anything! Just shut up and leave me alone!" Instead of apologizing to me, he tried to make it my fault. He accused me of not being supportive; he seemed resentful in a way that was confusing to me. There was little discussion beyond the angry words we hurled at each other because Stephen was not willing to say much else. I went to bed early, and Stephen went down to the lobby bar and then stayed there drinking.

Tomorrow's another day, I thought as I willed myself to go to sleep. *This weekend will give Stephen a break from work. He just needs a little time to himself.* Little did I know, Stephen was running out of time. No wonder he had been driving so fast. Later I would realize that he had been right to be worried and nervous.

CHAPTER FIVE
CLOSING IN

On Thanksgiving morning, we watched the parade. Stephen, who had drunk a lot the night before and had come to bed long after I'd gone to sleep, seemed happy and more relaxed. I tried to be happy too and shrug off Stephen's behavior and our arguments from the day before. After breakfast we all put on our coats and headed outside.

It was exhilaratingly cool out on the streets of Manhattan. The boys were happy and having a great time.

"Look Mom! Look!" Stephen Jr. chirped.

"Yes, I can see!"

It was a cold day, but we had a great viewing spot for the parade right on Madison Avenue. Stephen had Stephen Jr. on his shoulders, while I held our toddler, Ryan. Stephen reached for my hand as we stood watching. I took it and held it. We smiled at each other, a real smile. I understood it as his apology for the way he had acted the day before. I remember it as a reassuring moment; I so wanted everything to be good between the two of us.

On our drive back home after the parade, I replayed that moment again and again in my mind. For the first time in a long time, I felt like we had connected—if even for a moment—and it gave me another glimmer of hope. It was a much quieter ride than it had been on the way into the city, with the little conversation that took place focused on the boys and not between me and Stephen.

I was looking forward to Thanksgiving dinner at my parents' house that night. When we got home at noon, we unpacked the car and then, although it was cold and windy, Stephen challenged the boys to ride their bikes the eight blocks with him to my mother's house while I followed in the car. I was happy he wanted to spend that time with the boys. He loved bike riding with them and Ryan loved being in the seated bike attached to the back of Stephen's.

Although Stephen was still edgy, he was attentive to the boys, and there were pockets of time when he seemed to enjoy the festivities at Thanksgiving along with everyone else. He was someone who liked cooking now and then, so when he wasn't outside on the phone, he was usually in the kitchen helping out. My brothers and Stephen's dad were there for dinner, and it was great to see them and to visit with my aunt and uncle who were in from out of town. Everyone was socializing, getting caught up on all the family news, and enjoying each other's company.

One of my brothers—my twin brother—noticed how often Stephen left the table to go outside. He commented to me that Stephen was on the phone a lot and seemed distracted. I had noticed Stephen that kept going outside to smoke, but I was busy visiting with the rest of the family. I really did not want to see anything unusual in his behavior. Having to account for Stephen's behavior was becoming more and more of a chore, one that I didn't enjoy.

"It's his job," I told my brother. "It's a tough market, and things aren't easy for Stephen right now." My brother just shrugged. I was glad that my brother left it at that and didn't question me further, especially since I didn't have any satisfactory answers.

The fact that it was Thanksgiving made me think about how blessed I was and how much I had to be thankful for. Even though I was in turmoil, wondering what was upsetting Stephen so much and confused about our marriage, it was comforting to be with family. I felt grateful for all the good things in my life, particularly everyone in my family whom I loved so much. Although my parents had divorced, we all remained tight-knit.

After dinner and dessert, we said our good-byes. Since it was dark now, I drove home with the boys, leaving their bicycles at my mother's house, while Stephen raced ahead on his bike. Stephen had to be up at 4:00 AM. He was going deep-sea fishing with my uncle, who was staying with my parents for the weekend, and so we went to bed early. It had been a busy and eventful two days. I didn't know that we only had less than one day left as a full family. After that, our lives would never be the same.

The next morning, around 4:15 AM, Stephen left to pick up my uncle at my mother's house for their fishing trip. Stephen loved to fish. He had been fishing since he was a little boy. He loved the peace that came from being out on the open water and the thrill of actually catching a fish. It was absolutely one of his favorite things to do—a sport for him as much as a form of relaxation. He often went out on one of the many party boats based on Long Island's south shore, and he was delighted to take my uncle out on a fishing expedition that day.

I was glad that Stephen had such enthusiasm and hoped that a morning of fishing would help him relax and put him in a good frame of mind for the remainder of the weekend. Although I had felt a shift in our relationship over the last several months, I tried not to give in to the fact that our marriage was getting rockier and rockier. There were increasing moments of stress and anger between us, and mostly, I was confused. *What's happened to my best friend?* Lying in bed that morning, I thought, *What can I do to make things right?* We had stopped treating each other like best friends. The conversations between us were far and few between. He had stopped working out and no longer dressed nicely. I realized that I was becoming less and less attracted to him.

That morning, before Stephen left, he kissed me.

I sleepily told him, "Good-bye, have fun!" As I look back on that moment, that kiss was one of our last kisses that I really remember.

My uncle was ready and waiting, as eager for the fishing trip as Stephen was. Later, Rod told me that something odd had happened on their way to the fishing boat.

"That's weird," my uncle had said to Stephen. "It looks like that cop's following us."

The roads were deserted at 4:30 AM, except for a police car that was right behind them. The officer followed them all the way to the fishing boat. Rod was sure they were going to be pulled over for some minor infraction. He saw Stephen tense up, gripping the steering wheel, but once they got to the boat, Rod said that the police car passed them and kept on going. *Just a coincidence,* Rod thought as they pulled their gear out of the car and headed toward the fishing boat.

It turned out to be a wonderful morning on the ocean. They caught several fish, told a few tall tales, and had plenty of laughs. At about 12:30 PM, Stephen called me to say that they were back from fishing and had a great morning. He had just dropped my uncle off at my mother's house, two miles away from our house. He asked if I needed him to stop and pick up anything from the store, and I told him no, we were fine; he said he would be home in a couple of minutes.

The few minutes turned into an hour. When Stephen was still not home, I called him back but only reached his voicemail. I guessed he was delayed somehow. I thought perhaps he had decided to stop by the store anyway, or maybe he had stopped in somewhere to see a friend. I was a little puzzled though because he knew we had plans for that afternoon. We were supposed to spend the rest of the day with the boys at my mom's house, and then later we were to attend the wake for one of my best friends' mother. As more time went by and Stephen was still not home, I got annoyed. *What's up with him anyway?* I thought. I tried him again but still could not reach him.

It wasn't like him to be unavailable by cell phone. Why would he not answer? During those first few hours of not being able to reach him, I found myself getting angrier and angrier. How could he be so inconsiderate? Maria's mother had died, and we had her wake to go to! Why wouldn't he return my calls? I grew more and more furious by the minute.

However, when more than a few hours went by and I got the voicemail on his cell phone over and over again, I began to think something bad had happened to him. Something shifted in me, and I went from being angry to feeling anxious and nervous. I envisioned all sorts of scenarios. He was in a ditch somewhere, he'd had a heart attack behind the wheel, he'd been kidnapped, he'd been mugged and was unconscious, he'd gotten drunk and passed out and didn't know where he was. *What could have possibly happened for Stephen to just disappear like this?*

I put the boys in the car and drove the route between our house and my mother's house repeatedly—frantically looking for any sign of Stephen but remaining as calm as possible so as not to frighten the boys. I didn't tell them their father was missing. When we got back home, after searching and seeing no sign of him, I called anyone who might possibly know where Stephen was. I called his father, his sister, and his close friends. I called the hospitals and the local police, neither of whom seemed concerned. After giving a description of Stephen and the make of his car, they just replied in a very professional but brisk manner, "No. No one here of that description."

Where could he be? The tension was mounting, and I was in a panic. By evening, I was so nervous and beside myself that I just did not know which way to turn. It was miserable outside. The rain was coming down hard, and the wind was blowing, and I just kept pacing back and forth, looking out the window and running every scenario I could think of through my head. *Where in the world could Stephen be? Please, please just let him be alive!*

The phone was ringing constantly, but it was always

family or a friend wanting to know if Stephen had returned home or if there was any word from him.

I finally put the boys back in the car and drove them over to my mother's house, knowing that I was waiting for bad news. I did not want them to see my heightened anxiety—I could barely contain it at this point—and thought it was best for the boys not to be home when I received whatever phone call I was sure I would be getting. When I dropped the boys off, my mother tried to be supportive and offer ideas about where Stephen might be, but the truth was that everyone was just as baffled as I was. Stephen knew that we had to attend the wake and I was sure that he would never miss that, so I knew something was seriously wrong. I told my sons they were going to have a fun sleepover at Mimi's house with their aunt and uncle, and they were thrilled.

When I came back home, I called Stephen's best friend, and he helped me look for Stephen before I went to the wake. We drove around our town and neighboring areas, checking parking lots, restaurants, bars—any place that would make sense. Stephen's friend went with me to the funeral home, as he knew the family as well. The whole time we were there, I worried but did not tell anyone what was going on.

Some people asked where Stephen was, but I shrugged off the question by saying he just hadn't come home yet and I was sure he was okay. I didn't want to start any drama or divert any attention from my grieving best friend. We only stayed about an hour. After we left, we continued our search.

Stephen's friend was very accommodating and did all he could to help, including using his wonderful sense of humor to try and make light of the situation. After hours of searching, we finally gave up, as there was not a trace of Stephen. Without saying a word about it to each other, we knew something really bad had happened. Sometimes you just have that gut feeling, and your intuition tells you something's very wrong.

When I returned home to an empty house, I became even more unglued. I called my friends Brooke and Laura, and they came over to wait with me. They tried to calm me down, but I was frantic. We could not come up with any possible explanation that didn't make Stephen's disappearance a very bad situation. By this time, I was convinced my husband was dead. I thought maybe he had stopped for gas, gotten carjacked, and the whole situation had gone from bad to worse, quickly getting out of control somehow. My mind was reeling with possibilities. I paced around the house, from the den to the kitchen and back again, frantic and filled with full-blown anxiety. My friends sat on the couch in the den, doing their best to help calm me down. One minute I would be sobbing, the next I would snap out of it and just repeat to myself over and over, "He'll come home. He'll call. He'll come home. He'll call ..."

Finally, my friends and I moved to the kitchen and sat down around the table. Every time the phone rang, I jumped to get it, hoping it would be Stephen and not another concerned friend or family member wondering if I had heard anything yet. After hours of waiting, praying, crying, searching, and calling Stephen's cell phone every half hour only to get his voicemail, I finally received the telephone call I had dreaded.

It was nine o'clock. It had been nearly nine hours since I last spoke to Stephen.

The man on the other end of the phone, identifying himself as a Nassau County police officer, told me, "I have some bad news for you," and suggested that I sit down. I didn't. But, I probably should have.

CHAPTER SIX
THE WRONG MAN

Nothing could have prepared me for that call from the Nassau County police officer.

"What's happened? Where's my husband?" I pleaded desperately into the phone. I waited for him to say it. I thought I knew what he was going to say: *He's dead, Mrs. Trantel. We're so very sorry.*

"Your husband," the police officer said, "is in custody for a series of bank robberies that have occurred all over Nassau County."

"What?" I shrieked. "My husband? Stephen? This is a terrible mistake. You have the wrong man!" In the hours leading to this terrible moment, I anticipated all kinds of scenarios, but not this one.

This was absurd—a horrible mix up.

Stephen was not a bank robber. He was a trader on Wall Street. He was my husband. He was a dad.

They had the wrong man. However, the police officer insisted they had evidence that Stephen was who they had been looking for.

Stephen got on the phone himself.

"Steve, what's going on? What's going on? What's going on?"

"It's okay. I'm innocent." *I knew it!* I told him that I believed him.

"Of course you're innocent," I said. "How did this happen?"

Stephen told me that at 12:40 PM that afternoon, as soon as he had dropped off my uncle and hung up the phone with me, five Nassau County cop cars had stopped his truck and surrounded him, just a few hundred feet from my mother's home. No one, I later found out—not even neighbors—had seen it happen. He said had no idea what it was all about, but before he knew it, he was handcuffed and escorted into the backseat of an unmarked car.

"I got to the stop sign and five cops surrounded me. They handcuffed me and put me in the car. And I'm like, 'Guys, all this for a tail light? Come on.'" Earlier that day he'd realized that his tail light was out.

His tan Suburban, the truck he loved so much, was taken from the scene. It all took less than a minute.

Stephen had been driven to the police precinct where he was still being questioned. By law, the police were permitted to hold him without an attorney present for twelve hours. For the previous nine hours, he had been under interrogation.

He assured me, "Jeanne, they have the wrong person. It's not me." Of course it wasn't him! There wasn't a doubt in my mind. He told me to try not to worry and assured me he was going to get everything worked out. I trusted him completely.

The police officer returned to the phone and said they would be holding my husband overnight and to meet him for his arraignment the next morning at 9:00AM at the first district court in Hempstead. That was it. There was no further explanation. I was stunned as I listened to the phone line disconnect.

When I hung up the phone, my friends, Laura and Brooke, who had been sitting with me and heard my half of the conversation asked what in the world was going on. For a long time, I could not respond. I was absolutely paralyzed and so overwhelmed with shock that I could not get any words out. It was a very strange feeling, not being able to speak.

"They think Stephen is a bank robber," I finally said. "There has been some awful mistake. I have to meet him in court tomorrow morning." They were both as stunned as I was. Well, almost. I don't know how they could be as stunned as me. He was my husband, after all.

We actually spent a minute or two laughing at the ridiculousness of the accusation. "Who would possibly think Stephen Trantel is a bank robber? That's crazy!"

Stephen was a Little League coach and played Santa Claus at annual Christmas parties. He volunteered at soup kitchens and Habitat for Humanity. Also, who robs banks except in the movies? Do real people actually rob banks?

"It sounds so serial!"

"This only happens in the movies!"

The laughing subsided as quickly as it had begun. Though the three of us were absolutely convinced there had been a huge mistake and they had the wrong guy, the seriousness of the situation set back in.

We all agreed that I was in no condition to be alone. We decided I should pack an overnight bag and stay at Laura's house. I remember the three of us standing in my bedroom looking into the closet.

"This is unbelievable! I just can't understand the whole thing. And, what does one wear to an arraignment, anyway?" I asked. I think we may have laughed again in total disbelief. We all agreed that accusing Stephen of robbing banks was ridiculous. However, months would pass before I would feel like laughing about anything again.

At that point, standing in front of my closet, still trying to pick out an outfit for the next morning, I began to grow numb and felt myself distancing from my body, as if I was barely there. Stephen—my husband, my rock—was not coming home that night.

He was spending the night in a jail! Stephen was not a criminal! What a frightening mess this was!

It was incomprehensible to me. Somehow, I gathered up random items to throw in a bag and then called both my parents and Stephen's dad to tell them the little I knew.

I rode in silence to my friend's house, my mind racing and my body absolutely fatigued from the stress of the day. Laura continued to reassure me the whole ride, saying over and over again that there had been a mistake and it just couldn't be true.

Once we got to Laura's house, we woke up her husband, a good friend of Stephen's, and told him what was going on.

"No way it was Stephen," he agreed.

I found I could not settle down to sleep as I had

so much anxiety. Laura stayed up with me almost the entire night. We lit a candle to pray for Stephen, and I spent the whole sleepless night going back and forth between crying and praying. I really needed her support and company to get me through that long night; what a wonderful friend she was to me.

Later, I would find out that we had left my house just in time. I had just missed the media circus that showed up a short time after we had driven away. Reporters would camp out in front of my house for the next three days. Not only that, but they would be in my life, hounding me on and off, for the next six months.

The next morning, Stephen's father picked me up at Laura's house and drove us to the courthouse. My father and Stephen's best friend met us there. I had not slept for one minute the night before, and I assumed the same was true for everyone else as well. We spoke very little to each other. I guess there was a high anxiety level for all of us, as no one really knew anything at that point. We had no idea what to expect of the arraignment.

We were all there waiting in the courtroom when Stephen was brought before the judge in handcuffs. He looked terrible. He looked much smaller than his 5' 10" frame. I knew he had lost weight over the last few months, but seeing him standing there, I was taken aback by his whole demeanor. He was wearing the same clothes he had on when he went fishing— jeans, sneakers, and his NY Giants sweatshirt. He looked thin and tired, and—it actually crossed my mind—he looked like a criminal. I could not even focus on what was being said. It was brief. Bail was set at $500,000 cash, and that was it. Stephen was whisked away.

I could not believe what had happened right before my eyes. I kept asking questions of Stephen's father, his friend, and even my father. What was our next step? What were our options? Did Stephen tell them anything he hadn't told me? Was he hiding anything from me? Were they hiding anything from me? Couldn't we use the records of Stephen's trades to prove he was on the floor trading that day and not robbing a bank? Wasn't there some way to prove his innocence?

Stephen had a lawyer there, someone I had never met before. Even he could not shed any light on the situation, saying that at this point, he had nothing to speak to me about. That opened up the floor for a litany of other questions I had. Where in the world had this lawyer come from? How did he get his name and reputation anyway? Did he have any experience in this kind of situation? How long would Stephen need to stay in jail? Why was the bail set so high? How would we possibly raise the money?

Most frustrating of all was that there were so few answers for all of my questions.

"How can this be? What's the next step?" I asked. "How do we defend Stephen and correct such a horrible mistake?" No one had any answers for me. I felt completely helpless.

And, $500,000—that's half a million dollars. Where does one get $500,000? I stood next to Stephen's friend and cried.

An hour later, when I returned home after court, the media was waiting outside my front door. When my father and I pulled up and saw the TV trucks and reporters all over my yard, we did a U-turn right in the middle of my block. It would be four days before I dared try to go home again.

Those were four long days. I stayed at my mother's house with the boys because it felt much safer there and I wasn't ready to go home yet. The media was the last thing I wanted to deal with. I could barely speak as it was, let alone in front of a microphone or camera. Finally, after four days, I was starting to feel like a prisoner in my mother's house. Despite the media presence, it was time to go home. The boys needed to be back at our house in their own beds, and we needed to get back to some sort of sleep routine. The fatigue was taking its toll on all of us.

I told my older son, Stephen Jr., that his father had gotten into trouble with the police and it was going to take some time for the police to discover the truth and for everything to get worked out and cleared up.

"It'll be over soon," I said and as I said it I almost believed it. My three-year-old son, Ryan, was too young to understand the situation, so I didn't explain as much to him; I just let him know that his father would be home soon.

There was so much chaos and confusion with the media presence once we returned home, I decided to keep the boys home from school for a few days. The whole situation was so eerie; it felt like a death in many ways as I continued to tell the boys their father would be coming back home again soon. I was a total wreck, mustering every ounce of will I had to keep it together.

I tried to shelter myself as much the boys; I really did not even dare leave my house. I felt very scared, shamed, and trapped. It was almost as if I had been accused of committing a crime as well. After all, Stephen was my husband. Even though I was convinced of Stephen's innocence, the very fact of being accused was horrifying. We were good people; how could this happen to us? We went to church, paid our bills (or so I thought) and tried to live without hurting others. How could we be accused of something so awful? How could I explain that it was all some horrible mistake?

I didn't want anyone to see me. My friends encouraged me to go out, but I refused. They even went to the grocery store for me. I just could not do it. I was so ashamed of my situation, afraid of who I might run into. I always wondered who was looking at me or judging me. I was in total despair.

So much was going on that my head was spinning. With Stephen in prison and the boys and I alone in the house, the continual media presence heightened my anxiety. I could not even find any respite in my own home. Reporters and cameramen were at my door; they were calling on the phone and following me as I left the house.

"Mrs. Trantel! Can I talk to you for a minute? Mrs. Trantel! What do you think of all this? Did he do it? Mrs. Trantel! Did you know that your husband was robbing banks? How are you handling all of this? Mrs. Trantel!"

Those next few weeks are difficult to remember and

81

still a blur. I was worried about Stephen and the effect all of this was having on the boys; I could not think straight.

Friends came over all the time. They cooked dinner for us and brought food and money. The boys were utterly confused; they couldn't understand why everyone kept bringing us food and money. Realizing the boys needed time away from the chaos, more friends stepped in to help, having the boys over to their houses, or taking the boys away from the media circus on our block by bringing them to a park or somewhere else to play.

Our family and friends understood my need to get back to our routine and have a less chaotic home during the first weeks that Stephen was in jail awaiting bail, but they were kind enough not to leave us completely on our own during that traumatic time. Stephen's friends from the Exchange and people from our community continued to check in with me and offered to help with the boys whenever I needed assistance. Rockville Centre is an amazing town. The outpouring of care and support far outweighed any negativity or blame. We even had a prayer night at my house, and over forty people came to offer prayers and help for Stephen and my family. I was overwhelmed with the generosity and understanding shown to me and to my family. People were in and out of the house constantly, stopping by on a regular basis to check in, say hello, and see if we needed anything. My phone rang constantly, mostly with people who were trying to help. Our local weekly paper did a front-page story on Stephen the following Thursday, which stirred things up and kept people talking and speculating. My community was in shock. So many people knew Stephen and me and our extended families. Stephen was the "guy next door," a Little League baseball coach and very well liked, so everyone from town was in a state of disbelief.

CHAPTER SEVEN
SLOW AWAKENING

After a while, I had to request that friends come by the house less often; the constant commotion was just too much for the boys. They were scared, and though I did my best at the time, I wasn't as grounded as I would have liked to be. Ryan cried a lot at night and asked for his daddy. To this day, my older son Stephen remembers coming home and seeing piles and piles of food on the shelves and overflowing bags of groceries in our spare room. While I was really appreciative of our friends' thoughtfulness and generosity, it was time to get back to as regular a routine as possible and have a quiet house.

While Stephen was in Nassau County jail awaiting bail, I visited him regularly. He was allowed to have visitors three times a week, and though visiting times were split between me and his father, I was always given the first choice. On each visit, I continued to try to make some sense out of the situation. Going there was a frightening experience for me as I had not ever been to a jail before. I never imagined I would be standing in line to see my husband, who was literally "behind bars."

The Nassau County jail is a rundown, terrible institution where visitors are made to feel like criminals and are subjected to racial taunts and insults from guards and staff. Just going through the process to get into the waiting room is very intimidating and a traumatic ordeal. I can still remember the smell – almost like being in a hospital, but with an underlying odor of sweat. Visitors had to sign in at a small portable house outside the jail before entering. I was treated badly there by the guards, as were all of the other visitors. There wasn't a lot of compassion for any of us. One guard in particular (I can still picture him— very tall with red hair) was especially rude. Whenever I asked him a question, he would avoid eye contact with me and answer with so few words and such an unhelpful response, he might as well not have answered me at all.

During one particular visit, a woman who was waiting in line in front of me was all of a sudden thrown to the ground and arrested. The dogs leaped at her legs, and the guards shoved me out of the way.

The woman had been carrying drugs in her mouth to smuggle in to the person she was visiting. It was an awful, ugly scene, and I was really upset by the time I got in to see Stephen. Everything about that place was disturbing and I needed some reassurance from him that everything would be okay. When I saw him though, he looked awful. He was thin and looked completely disheveled. It was a profound moment because, for the first time, I started to realize that he couldn't help me at all. I couldn't rely on him. He could barely help himself. For a moment, I was furious that I had to visit that horrible place and witness all this craziness because of him. After that visit, I cried the whole way home. It was during that visit that I began to wonder if Stephen and I were going to make it as a married couple. That day, in the visiting room, Stephen felt more like a stranger to me than the husband, friend and lover he'd been for years in our marriage.

Such things only happened in the movies! What kind of place was this? I wanted to be as far away from a place like that as possible. I just couldn't understand how in the world our lives had come to this.

Stephen looked worse and worse every time I visited

him. On another particular visit, I was seated across from him in the visiting room and thought to myself, *I don't even recognize my own husband.*

I leaned closer to him and asked, "Stephen, what's that smell?"

With tears in his eyes, he said, "It's me. I don't dare take a shower. You don't know what it's like in here … how bad it really is." I had never seen him look so vulnerable, and so very, very scared.

Stephen acted strangely during my visits. He almost acted…guilty. It was difficult to talk to him while he was there, as there really wasn't any privacy by phone or in person. Our visits were strained and our conversations were very vague and distant. Stephen kept professing his innocence, saying not to worry and that things would be cleared up, but his avoidance of my questions and his secrecy were more reflective of a guilty man's behavior. His whole demeanor made me uneasy. However, I believed in his innocence. At least, I wanted to. With all my heart, I wanted to. He was a good man and I couldn't understand how he had ended up in this horrible place.

In the beginning, I was certain that Stephen would be exonerated very quickly. I thought he could use his trading records to show he had been working during the times the robberies occurred. In fact, Stephen had even mumbled a promise to me that he would work on getting those records. However, I soon learned that Stephen had not been working on the floor of the Exchange in months. Some of his work friends came by the house to tell me how long it had been since they had seen him on the floor. How could that be? I had packed his lunch and then given it to him as he left to catch the train. Others mentioned seeing and talking to Stephen in town at times when I believed that he had been at the Exchange working. The calls I had received during the last few months from the mortgage company and utility companies about late payments now seemed more ominous.

As I did my research about the string of robberies, I discovered a picture of the supposed bank robber that appeared in *Newsday*, our Long Island paper, on Thanksgiving Eve.

"Have You Seen This Man?" the story read. According to the article, the camera at the ATM machine in the vestibule of one of the banks had snapped a profile picture of a man who was accused of a number of bank robberies on Long Island. Upon examination, I thought the person in the photo, although in disguise, really did resemble Stephen.

Could this be a case of mistaken identity? I asked myself. Was that the reason he was arrested? But, as I recalled Stephen's behavior when I visited the real estate office before our trip to the city, it seemed to play out a frightening scenario. As I searched my memory of that morning, I realized that the reason Stephen so quickly closed the newspaper when my son and I walked in was because he had actually been reading that very *Newsday* article. And he had been looking at a photo of himself.

I continued to ask Stephen some of my questions when I visited him, but he still had no good answers. He kept saying it was just a case of mistaken identity and that I needed to leave it to him—everything would be cleared up and we'd be fine. As for the photos that had been obtained in the banks, he again said, "It's not me!" Repeatedly, Stephen just kept saying that he was taking care of things and it would all be worked out.

Stephen's father was a retired police officer; surely, he could clarify this whole situation, I thought. Unfortunately, even he knew very little during that time and never had any new information to share with me. And my father, an attorney, had worked as a federal prosecutor. How ironic was all of this? My father offered his legal expertise, but Stephen kept him shut out.

Even though I knew from visiting Stephen that he could barely take care of himself at the time, I was still hoping that, somehow, Stephen would take care of the situation and then be able to take care of us again. I realize I was not strong then. I was still looking to him for direction, still hoping he would eventually be able to help me and the boys through the trauma we were living. I had always depended on him and did not know my own capabilities.

I never had the opportunity to speak with Stephen's lawyer, and I was never questioned by the police. I had been told by Stephen not to speak with his attorney, and when I did see him at the courthouse, he was completely unapproachable. Stephen confided in his best friend and his father and chose not to speak to me about most things. I was kept totally in the dark.

My cousin, Lisa, flew in from Chicago to help me out during that time. She was my angel—an amazing person. Lisa was full of energy, with a quick wit and a commanding personality. The boys loved her, and so did I. Lisa cooked, cleaned, and quickly took control of the house. One afternoon, I returned home to find she had torn up the old living room and dining room carpet and had scrubbed and polished the floors beneath. This was a project Stephen and I had been meaning to do.

"Do you like it?" Lisa asked. It was a beautiful surprise for me. Lisa even painted my son's room and did a plumbing repair. It seemed she could do just about anything and everything. She was constantly busy and helped keep my spirits up, even when I was at some of my lowest points.

"Don't worry. You're going to get through this," she said more than once.

In the meantime, the media was still hounding me, keeping me totally on the defensive. I was frightened and upset by their intrusion into our lives, but it made Lisa angry. She would go head to head with them, hollering at them to go away and even chasing them out of the yard. She hung towels up against the windows to prevent them from looking in. My kitchen looked so odd with all those towels hanging, but it worked! There were many times when I felt like crying, but Lisa made me smile instead. Lisa is a funny person, and she had a way of cutting through all the thick tension and lightening the mood in our house.

I was particularly grateful to people like Lisa—who were able to make the boys and me laugh at times—because it was heart wrenching to see what the boys were going through during this whole period in our lives. As a mother, of course, I felt their pain;

it was heartbreaking to see them suffering. They were confused and scared because their lives had been turned upside down overnight and they didn't understand what had happened. They had never seen the media in person and had never been in the media themselves, so it was terrifying for them. I tried to explain to them what was going on and kept telling them Daddy would be home soon. They adored their father, and they desperately wanted him home. I reassured them, as Stephen reassured me, that everything would be settled, and soon.

A few weeks after he had been arrested, Stephen called me from the jail one day, terribly distraught, and said he wanted to kill himself.

"I just can't take it anymore. I just want to die," he said.

"That's crazy! I'm coming right now, I'll get there as soon as I can." I was frightened for him and rushed over in a terrible snowstorm to visit him. Since it was during a blizzard, no one else was on the road. Still, the trip which normally was half an hour took me an hour because of the terrible road conditions on the way the jail. When I got to the jail, the correction officers were kinder to me than they had ever been. The jail was eerie, as no one else was there. We talked for a long while until Stephen seemed to pull himself together again—but he continued to profess his innocence. We talked a lot about the children.

"How are they doing?" he asked.

"They're hanging in there. It's hard, but they're okay."

"They're good boys."

"Yes, they are." I told him all about the media and what was going on at home and in Rockville Centre. I told him about all the people who had come over and helped me and the boys in one way or another.

"I've got to tell you, I'm really scared," he admitted. He explained what it was like to be living in jail, the lack of privacy, the dirtiness, the bad food. He told me that he felt like an animal in jail. It was never quiet and one always had to watch one's back. He was surrounded by guys who had done some really violent things. He said he had no idea how this happened, how his life had changed so dramatically. One minute he was sleeping in bed next to me with the boys close by and the next minute he was sleeping in a jail cell.

The guards, who normally were very invasive, left us alone. We talked and held hands and looked up at the snow through the windows. I remember feeling reassured. Stephen was innocent and he was going to come home to me and the boys and life was going to be good. It was the nicest time we'd spent together since Stephen's incarceration; it was a moment of connection, a moment of true intimacy. The bars seemed to melt away for a little while and it was if were back on the beach together, walking along the sand, just the two of us, or playing cards and laughing together the way we had when we'd first gotten married. Later he wrote me a letter thanking me for that visit and for loving him.

I asked him as many questions as I could on my visits.

"Where are your trading records? Since you were working on the floor, why can't they help us clear this whole thing up?"

"Why would they arrest an innocent man? Are you really innocent? How long are they going to keep you here?"

"What happened during those nine hours they interrogated you? What did they ask you? What did you say to them? Why won't you tell me?"

"Is prison as bad as people say it is? Are other inmates picking on you? Do you sleep at all?"

"How did you get your attorney? How are we going to pay for that?"

He told me that he hardly slept at all. Other than

that, I never got any straight answers from him. I left every visit frustrated and confused. Why wasn't he talking to me?

I needed to know more about what was going on and wanted to believe Stephen. No, it was more than that. I really *did* believe him when he said he was innocent. I had to; he was my husband, my best friend. How could I not believe in him, the man who had taken care of me for so many years? But, as I read and watched news stories about the bank robberies, more and more questions were on my mind.

The headlines read, "Suspect Nabbed in Robberies," "Double Life," "Family Man Also Bank Robber," and "Heist Suspect Cast as Man of Integrity"—all with varying amounts of details about Stephen's background and his arrest. The stories were convincing in portraying Stephen as a bank robber. They painted a picture of a man who walked into several banks and very politely robbed them.

Each day there would be some new development, some small piece of information related to Stephen and the bank robbery story, and none of it was encouraging.

Nothing was making any sense. I was discovering that there were many things about which Stephen had not been truthful. The news was blasting the story everywhere, and everyone was starting to find out more and more details through what was being reported. Even when I questioned Stephen about what I was finding out, he managed to stay in control.

"Don't worry about it. I'm handling things with my lawyer."

"What can I do?" I asked him.

"There's nothing you can do. Just relax. It'll all work out."

CHAPTER EIGHT
CONFESSION

Stephen spent three weeks in jail before bail was raised for him to be released. It was difficult to raise the $500,000 in cash, but Stephen's father took a mortgage on his house. Stephen's cousin, friends, and other family members were also very generous and contributed what they could. We were all relieved to have Stephen out before Christmas. In the back of my mind, I had a feeling this might be the boys' last Christmas with their father for a long time.

I did not go to pick him up when he was released on bail; his father did. By then, I was starting to believe that Stephen had been deceiving me and might actually be guilty of robbing all those banks. It was horrifying to come to the realization that the man I loved, the father of my children, might be lying to me and may have ruined our lives with desperate, stupid acts. Could he have done such a thing? How could I not have known? A few days before Stephen was released on bail, it was my father who was finally able to get me to sit down and take a hard look at the situation. My father is a very straightforward man. He can be intimidating, but I have so much respect for him as he is also very honest and loyal. As an attorney with plenty of contacts, he had done a better job than I had of uncovering the facts of Stephen's case and had learned of the evidence against him.

On a day when the children were out of the house, my father sat me down in the living room and said we needed to talk.

"Jeanne, it doesn't look good for Stephen. I'm afraid he hasn't been honest with you," he said. "There seems to be considerable evidence against him." It was then that he told me that he knew for sure that Stephen was guilty. I cried and cried. While my rational side understood and believed my father, I was still hoping that Stephen was innocent and that there was some other explanation. It just could not be. How could I have been so deceived? And, by the man I had known and loved for twelve years?

I kept asking my father if he was sure—*positively* sure—though with his background in law enforcement, a part of me knew he was telling me the truth. He had spoken to the police, asked a lot of questions, and had gotten enough answers to know that his son-in-law was guilty. Though there was a part of me that now knew Stephen had done what he had been accused of, I still needed to hear it straight from Stephen to believe it fully.

I was unable to confront Stephen in any meaningful way while he was in jail because he refused to have much discussion about the case, saying that the jail was wired and there were tape recorders everywhere. I assumed that was why he barely answered any of the questions I kept throwing at him during those weeks. Now that he was out, I hoped we could finally have a candid and intimate conversation ... as soon as I was ready to.

Stephen stayed with his father that first night after being released, as I did not want him to come home right away. I was fearful of the media becoming a problem again, and I felt betrayed and confused. I was angry and in a lot of pain; I just didn't want him in the house yet. The thought of sharing the same bed with him was unacceptable.

I felt like I needed time to sort things out in my head, whereas he just wanted to put the whole thing in the past and have us move on. It was scary to me that, at times, he could think this whole situation was just not that big of a deal.

"It's over," he actually said when he got out of jail. "It's in the past."

He came home the following night, and we finally talked face to face. I was ready, as I felt our home was a "safe" environment. After we put the boys to bed, we sat down in the living room, side by side on our couch. He tried to touch me and I pushed him away. His touch was no longer comforting to me.

I looked at him—looked right into his eyes—and said, "Stephen, you have to tell me the truth. You have to tell me everything. Did you rob all those banks?"

Stephen got up and started pacing back in forth in the living room. He didn't speak for a very long time. I waited quietly.

"Yes, Jeanne," he said with his voice trembling. "I did. I did what I am accused of. I robbed those banks. And I might have to go to prison."

There it was. I finally heard the truth from Stephen. It was what I had been suspecting for the last several days, but still, I was unprepared for the reality that hit me in that moment. I felt like all of the air had been taken out of my lungs. There were a hundred questions

I wanted to ask, but for a longtime I was speechless. How could my best friend have done this and then lied to me for so long about it? It was a life-altering moment for me. I had another out-of-body experience as I felt a part of me pulling away from myself, not wanting to be there in that room and in that conversation. I felt like I couldn't even comprehend all that he was saying.

Things had obviously not gone well for him while renting a seat on the Exchange and trading crude oil with his own money. Passing the wreckage of the Twin Towers each day was very depressing. Then came the death of his mother. His mother had been sick for nearly five years. The last three months of her life were excruciatingly painful for him. Stephen was torn between his desire to spend as much time as he could with his mother and making a go of it as an independent trader. The market was tough. Stephen said he was distracted, in mourning for his mom, and under pressure to provide for his family. He told me that he lost the mental edge that had kept him sharp in his trading. He began losing money. Lots of money.

Stephen said he borrowed from the Exchange and everyone he knew—his father, his sister, my mother, and even his friends. But he lost it all. He knew he was in trouble professionally, as trading was the only thing he knew how to do. He was literally stuck between a rock and a hard place. He knew he needed another career, another way to make a living, so he tried to branch out and consider other options. Even when he had three jobs (a donut business, a real estate agent, and a floor trader), he was not making money at any of them. Money was going out, but nothing was coming in. He was in a panic. He didn't feel like he could ask me to go back to work. He needed to be the sole provider for his family; to not be able to, especially when he'd been able to in the past, felt like the ultimate failure.

His state of mind and financial position were in such bad shape that eventually he began pretending to go to work. When his commodities credit line was exhausted and he was told to leave the Exchange, it crushed him. He knew his back was against the wall. Still, even then he could not admit this crisis to me.

"Why should both of us have to suffer?" he told me later he had rationalized. "You didn't need to know how bad things were."

He said he just *couldn't* tell me he was no longer at the Exchange and thought he could figure something out. However, as hard as he tried, he could not come up with any solution and felt there was nowhere else to turn. Stephen said he was desperate. That is when he knew he had to do something else—and quickly.

He remembered the moment exactly. It was early May 2003. It had been two months since he last worked, and we were literally broke. He couldn't pay the mortgage, the utility bills, the tuition for Ryan's preschool, the family's medical insurance, car insurance … the list went on. Meanwhile, I didn't have a clue how much it cost to maintain our lifestyle. In retrospect, I know that I should have known. I just didn't make enough effort to get involved. In that way, I failed him, my children and myself. It hurts me to think that my husband didn't feel he could come to me with his problems. I'm angry with myself for not forcing Stephen to tell me what was really going on. I let him lie to me for months. I let him get away with not giving me straight answers.

That day he was sitting in his truck outside the local library, only a few miles from home. Since I was at home in the mornings with our youngest son, he needed to be somewhere else. He wanted to be somewhere he could have peace and quiet, somewhere he would be left alone and no one he knew would see him. After all, he was supposedly at work in Manhattan.

He sat in his truck staring out the window, an

overwhelming sense of desperation taking over. Since losing his job on Wall Street, he had already borrowed money from his father and from his sister—and then lost it all. He got the license to sell real estate and had attempted to start the donut business, but nothing was working. He had lost so much money on the commodities exchange floor that he was barred from trading there anymore. There was no more money to trade anyway.

Having believed he had explored every other sane avenue, he thought, *I've got to steal money. If I can just get enough to pay the bills, I'll be able to get out of this hole. I have to get the money from somewhere. There is no other way.*

That's when the idea first came to him, sitting alone in the truck—he would rob a bank. He convinced himself there would be no victims if he robbed a bank; no one would get hurt, and it wouldn't be personal. He would be robbing an institution—not a person, he told himself. And he could get the money he needed quickly. If he was going to get away with it, he thought, he had to do it right. He went inside the library.

In a space tucked away in a private part of the library, he began his methodical research. Every day for the next several weeks, he read all he could on the subject. He scoured through Web sites that might offer relevant information he would need to know in order to pull it off successfully. He read books on the subject, newspaper articles about bank robberies, and police reports that detailed the incidents. Throughout this research, he was especially attentive to the specific ways that people had been caught. Eventually, he came up with a plan.

From some of his research on the Internet, Stephen had found out that the getaway car was what led to most people's arrest. He would be smart. He would be careful to leave the car parked several blocks away. He wouldn't make a run for it; he would casually make his way back to the car after robbing the bank. The rest of his plan would be precise and exact as well.

He diligently scouted locations. He told me about surveying the exterior by first driving and then walking a wide radius around each bank. He considered various entry and escape routes; he needed a location he could get away from quickly. He also needed there to be a place close by where he could change into his disguise; an isolated back alley with dumpsters—large enough for him to jump into—would be ideal.

He would then go into the bank to view the layout and the position of the cameras. Of course, there would always be cameras; there was no way around that. He would wear a disguise and would be careful to keep his head down to avoid being clearly seen. That he could do. However, if the bank had a guard or bulletproof glass at the teller window, it would be eliminated as a target, and he would move on to find another more suitable location. He especially didn't want to deal with a guard.

Once he had finally chosen a bank, he studied the bank to determine the best time to pull off the robbery. He did not want to be in the bank during peak traffic hours, and he was careful to be clear of the bank at a time when a high percentage of men, especially construction workers and laborers, were apt to be cashing their paychecks. He feared that if they were somehow alerted to a robbery in progress, those bank customers were the most likely to try and be the hero and stop him. That would be bad, as he didn't want any confrontation.

Choosing the right neighborhood, the most opportune time of day, and the best day of the week were all critical elements to success. Stephen discovered that police officers tended to go into banks on Wednesdays to cash their paychecks, so he avoided that day of the week. Friday was payday for most people, and a lot of those people went straight to the bank to cash their checks. There would be a lot of cash in the bank teller's drawer on a Friday afternoon. With each bank he surveyed, he made detailed mental notes about the traffic patterns in and out of the bank. Eventually, low-traffic and high-traffic patterns emerged, and he had the last piece of information he needed.

Each night at home, he would wait until I—who always went to bed early—and the children were asleep. He would go down to the basement and lock the door. Careful to put on latex gloves first, he would write down all of the observations he had mentally recorded during the day as he scouted the different banks. Later, when he no longer needed the piles of detailed notes, he shredded them and threw them away.

Knowing it was crucial to remain calm and in control at all times, and armed with hours of research that had educated him about how not to get caught, he was ready to put his plan into action.

It was July 2003, two months after his initial decision to act. Stephen drove his truck to within a few blocks of his target and parked in a nearby lot. The bank was close to a parkway, so he would have a quick escape route afterwards. Before entering the bank, he stopped in an alleyway across the street and changed into the disguise he would wear during the robbery. His disguise was simple—a wig with a baseball hat drawn low over his face, a fake moustache, and dark sunglasses. He slipped larger clothes on over his own, and was sure not to forget to put on the latex gloves. He left an empty coffee cup next to the dumpster in the alleyway. He would pick it back up on his return, so that after the robbery he could be seen as an innocent bystander who had stopped nearby for coffee. Who would ever suspect that the bank robber was strolling past, in plain sight, with a cup of coffee?

Although Stephen had researched and carefully planned for weeks, nothing had prepared him for the actual desperation, guilt, and terror he felt the very first time he opened the bank door and approached the teller's station. He picked out the teller that he felt was the weakest. He stood in front of the bank teller and passed the woman a piece of paper.

"Give me all your money," the handwritten note read. "I have a gun."

There was no gun, but he knew that the threat of one was enough. The teller, who looked terrified, handed the money over the counter. He took the money, put it in a brown paper bag, and then put the bag inside his oversized jacket. He took the note back and put it in his pocket. Then it was autopilot.

Walking out through the bank again was a blur. Somehow he made it to the alleyway. This was the first time he moved quickly—past a normal, steady walk—since putting his plan into motion. Once in the alleyway, he jumped into the large dumpster and took off the disguise, including the outer layer of clothes. Before leaving the alleyway, he picked up the coffee cup he had left there. Then he casually strolled around the corner and slowly made his way back to the car.

I want to be seen looking like a regular guy just walking to my car, he thought. Now that the disguise was off and the coffee cup was in his hand once again, he only had to make it to the car. Then he could calm down. No one chased him, and no one saw.

Stephen was amazed at how easy it was. It had taken only a few minutes.

He counted the money. The take was $11,000, the biggest take from what would end up being a total of ten robberies. He drove all over from town to town to secure money orders with the stolen money. He didn't want any type of paper trail. Some of the bills he owed were for relatively small amounts, so he could pay those with cash, but for the larger ones, he had to use money orders. With the bills paid, he felt be back on his feet, able to start over. He thought it was over.

However, it turned out that all the first robbery accomplished was to buy him some time. Before long, not more than a month later, the money was gone and the bills were piling up once more. It was a constant game of catch up. Almost as soon as the money came in, it went out again. The high mortgage payment was once again overdue, and the debt collectors were calling again. Nothing had changed. He still did not have a job or any way to make a living. He felt that he had no choice but to do it again. He felt that the second time would be even easier than the first. So began the cycle that lasted for five months.

Our night in New York for my birthday at the end of the summer was paid for by money he'd stolen during his second robbery.

In another robbery, Stephen would put the money he had stolen in the pocket of his pants, and ink would eventually explode on him. That night, he went to his family's cabana at the nearby beach club to wash all the dye off the money in the shower. He lost a lot of the money that time, and so he needed to get to another bank—quickly.

Another time, Stephen saw a baby in a baby carriage

next to someone who was standing in line in front of him at the bank he was about to rob. He thought of his own boys and felt desperately sad and guilty. But there were piles of bills that needed to be paid, and so he followed through with the robbery.

Yet another time, he robbed a bank that was right by where his mother-in-law worked, extremely nervous that he might run into her.

Once, he saw his aunt going into a bank he had already scouted out and decided on; he changed his mind about targeting that one.

With each robbery, he was meticulously careful to wear latex gloves when writing the note he used to demand the money from the teller and whenever handling that paper the note was written on. Except once. Just one time, he would hastily tear the piece of paper from his notebook without first putting on the latex gloves. It would be one of the few times he didn't take the note back from the teller and put it safely back in his pocket. This began the end of the five-month cycle of robbing banks.

Stephen told me that he believed if he stole enough money to pay our bills, he could get back on his feet. He was hoping that some of the deals he was working on at the real estate office would soon be coming to fruition. The bottom line was that he needed money and had run out of time. Stephen said he had decided that the best way to get cash—fast cash—was rob a bank. And that's exactly what he did. Ten times.

Without consulting me.

I cried the whole time he talked. I listened to him, and although I heard every word he said, I could not comprehend what he was telling me. I realized that Stephen had driven like a maniac that day on our way to Manhattan because he was sure the police were following him into the city, and he was doing his best to outrun them—with me and the boys in the car. I had been involved in a getaway attempt without realizing it.

I was so incredibly sad and kept asking him, "Why? Why would you do that?" I couldn't understand why he hadn't come to me and told me we were broke. Why hadn't he explained that we were out of money? The fact that he would rob banks as a way to make a living was too much to wrap my brain around. I looked at him, thinking to myself, *Who is he? Where did my husband go? What happened to the man I married? The father of my children?*

Stephen finally spoke again. He said that many

times he had thought of telling me the truth. He'd come close once when we had been out in Montauk.

That night, Stephen had planned to tell me what he had been doing, but when the time came, he simply couldn't do it. The more he thought about it, the more he realized that if he told me, then I would be implicated. I would become an accessory if I knew, and if he was caught, we might both go to jail—and the kids would have no parents.

I was stunned. My mind was racing now. It had been three weeks since he was arrested, and it had taken this long for him to tell me? I begged again for another explanation.

"Stephen, how could you? Why this? How could you have done this, Stephen?"

He would only say, "Jeanne, I did it for us."

CHAPTER EIGHT
BETRAYAL

I was in shock. Stephen's admission sent me reeling again. At first, what I felt was sadness—deep sorrow for Stephen, the boys, and me. I still loved my husband. You don't just turn off years of loving someone, I found out, but the life I knew and loved was definitely over.

Though he lost even more weight and was clearly nervous about his fate and what was going to happen to him in jail, Stephen didn't seem to realize how much trouble he was in. Or, perhaps, he just did not want to face it. Maybe it was his way of coping, but he kept insisting that I forgive him.

"You have to forgive me and put it in the past," he said. To me, that was ridiculous. How could we put something in the past that was now determining our future as a couple and as a family? He said he did not want to lose his family, he would change, and he could make things right. But I knew it was too late for that.

The realization slapped me in the face. Not only had he been lying to me, Stephen had actively deceived me. He would get up every morning, get dressed, say good-bye to the kids and me, and then rob a bank—or spend his day planning to rob a bank.

So many incidents came to mind. Our trip to Wisconsin which had taken place a few days after the first robbery. Stephen's reluctance to have me use his truck for the trip I took September with my girlfriend. The jailbird costumes at Halloween. I remembered the red dye all over the floor of the shower of the beach cabana that turned out to be from ink that had exploded on stolen money, which Stephen had tried to wash off. The secret phone conversations that Stephen had told me were about work were not about his work as a commodities trader after all. Thanksgiving Eve and Thanksgiving Day, he had been on the phone to his attorney, pretty sure that the police were closing in. And, I was totally floored when I learned that our son's own knapsack became a major piece of evidence, as it proved to be the hiding place for the latex gloves that Stephen had used during the robberies.

I found out that our phones had been tapped, and

I was followed for quite a while before Stephen's arrest. Perhaps that was why I was never questioned. The police knew from my activities and phone conversations that I was totally unaware of what Stephen was doing.

The more I thought about it, the more all the puzzle pieces fell into place and started to make sense, showing me the big picture for the first time. I thought back to Stephen taking extra days off work here and there and not seeming to think twice about it. He had lost his appetite long before and had started caring less and less about his appearance. He'd stay up very late every night and sometimes not come to bed at all.

As I came to grips with the fact that Stephen really was a bank robber, and as more and more of his deceptions became apparent, I became very confused. How could the man I love have done such things? Had I ever known him at all? What else had he done that I had not known about?

It made me question our whole relationship. Is Stephen the man I always thought he was, or is he just a very good actor? Has our marriage been on the up and up, or have there been deceitful things going on all along?

These were some of the many thoughts going through my mind at the time. I was not sure which parts of my life were real and how much of a secret life Stephen had. Talk about turmoil; I knew I was betrayed, but I was totally bewildered at how this had been going on behind my back.

The truth, I finally admitted to myself, was that it had been over two years since I had really seen Stephen happy. I had known that something was wrong the last several months because he had been in a state of high anxiety, but September 11, 2001, was the start of Stephen's decline. As of that day, although I never knew it, we were literally broke. We had pushed ahead with our dreams—but in the end, they were unattainable.

It was Christmas time 2003, and I experienced such a mixture of feelings. During this time, my emotions went back and forth from sadness to uncertainty. I became more and more disillusioned with life, felt more and more betrayed. I had barely eaten or slept while Stephen was in jail, and I made my way through the day in a daze. I had no energy. It seemed I accomplished very little each day, and every time I turned around there was an obstacle to face. The severity of our financial problems became apparent quite quickly. We had no money. *How would we survive?* I had not had a full-time job or paid bills in years. We had two little boys to look after and a mortgage.

Stephen's arrest stayed big news in the community, and our family had now become the talk of the town. I struggled to hold my head high, even though I was pretty sure what people were saying. I was so ashamed of our circumstances and of what Stephen had done; I did not even want to leave the house. I did not know how I would ever face the world or what was ahead for us as a family.

It was the darkest time in our lives, a time when gossip and speculation could easily have taken over and led me even deeper into despair. Amazingly, it was instead a time where friendships and acts of kindness prevailed. Most people decided not to judge; instead, they were compassionate. The generosity continued.

Presents appeared in the mailbox. Someone left us a Christmas tree. Neighbors came over with bags of groceries. A dear friend stopped by and insisted I take the $500 she handed me. I remember the two of us crying in my kitchen. Several times in the next few months, men from the Commodities floor knocked on the door and left me envelopes with gifts of money. My friend Karen came over, paid the three months arrears on my mortgage, and later paid for my visit to the doctor when I was ill and had no medical insurance. My parents started to pay the mortgage going forward.

One day a group of people I knew came over and asked for my bills. They divided them up and each took one home to pay.

Friends came over to sit with me, to listen, or to watch my children. Every day, someone called with a kind word. There was such an outpouring of compassion and support from the people of my town, that even in my despair, I felt appreciative and blessed. It was also very surprising that the boys were not subjected to even one incident of ridicule or gossip while in school. The school staff and other parents were wonderful. They must have been great role models for their children, as my boys never had any problems from the other children. There were many moments of full-blown miracles for my boys and me to survive. Dealing with so many mixed emotions was completely overwhelming to me.

All these selfless acts were not just from people I knew. Some were strangers, and they were from all walks of life. They did not judge us. Or, at least not the boys and me. It seemed they all just wanted to help.

I started to look inward at the person I was. Had I been living such a shallow life? I was happy with my life as a wife and mother. I had remained ignorant of our finances. I was grateful to have had a husband with a career that afforded me the luxury of being with our sons full time. I didn't ask a lot of questions, even when bill collectors called the house. I realized, perhaps for the first time, just how much luxury I had been living in, as well as ignorance.

I had never known how much money it took to run our house, and I never really worried about it. Stephen had always given me an allowance for groceries and other things we needed throughout the month, but he paid all the bills and took care of everything else. I liked it that way and allowed Stephen to control our finances. *Even so, when things were going so badly, why didn't Stephen come to me and let me know that we were having problems? Why hadn't he simply asked me to get a job, something I would have willingly done? Why had he resorted to this? Was there too much pressure on Stephen to provide for us? Was I contributing to that pressure?*

I struggled and struggled to understand why. One minute I was blaming him, the next minute I was blaming myself. I began to realize that it wasn't just Stephen who needed to change. I needed to change as well.

Although Stephen spent Christmas Day at the house, he went back to his father's house for the next few weeks. For the moment, until we sorted some things out, I could not bear having him home. My heart was twisted and my thoughts were scattered. I was so emotional that I told Stephen I just could no longer have him live with us as my husband.

However, eventually Stephen came back to the house to spend his last few months with the boys. As tough as things were, he told me, it was better for him to be home with them and to try to get back to some type of normalcy. Stephen wanted to spend as much time with his sons as possible, knowing that soon he might be missing their day-to-day lives for a number of years. I finally consented and Stephen moved back into the house, in January 2004, still not sure of his future.

"Thanks Jeanne. We'll get through this," he said.

"I'm doing it for the boys," I responded. Once Stephen came home, the amount of people who came by started to diminish. I think some friends who did come probably felt awkward. I thought that most people would be judgmental about the situation we were in; after all, Stephen had brought this on himself. That was generally not the case. Most people were very cordial and helpful. Although no one condoned Stephen's behavior, our friends and family stood by us. Still, it was an incredibly difficult situation for all of us.

I knew I had to pull myself together. I decided to get

myself into a career where I could work close to home and have the flexibility to raise my boys, especially if I was raising them alone. I had never worked real estate before, but it seemed like a good option. Although Stephen had never made any sales, I resolved to get my real estate license and give it a try. I had been attending school to become a licensed massage therapist, and kept that going as well. Having Stephen home to take care of the boys made it easier for me. Even with so many acts of kindness and generosity, we were way behind in our bills. Our remaining car was towed away; our cell phones and house phones were all cut off for lack of payment. Yet, as terrible as things were, they were about to get worse.

Stephen would not be going to trial. The evidence against him was solid, and a trial would only prolong the inevitable and add to the financial hardship for us and for our families. There was evidence of Stephen's fingerprint on one of the notes handed to a teller. Apparently, when Stephen had torn a page from a notebook, he had left a print that was matched to a record for a DWI charge against him in 1984, from when he was still a teenager. This DWI charge was another thing I had known nothing about.

Stephen and his lawyer agreed that he would plead

guilty and go to prison. There was no way around it. Stephen's attorney told him that the sentence could be nineteen years. To us, that seemed like a lifetime, and we both agreed it was an unbearable amount of time.

At first, Stephen contemplated suicide.

"I should just kill myself," he said. "Then you, Stephen and Ryan could at least get some insurance."

"Don't be crazy."

One of his friends offered to help him "disappear" to Mexico. Because of the boys, he could not go through with either plan. Stephen said he would not leave behind a legacy of a criminal father who had "disappeared" or committed suicide. He felt he needed to serve his time and eventually have the chance to redeem himself for his sons. I agreed with him. More than anything, I wanted my boys to have a father they could look up to again rather than be ashamed of.

After much negotiation and discussion with his attorney and his father, on March 23, 2004, Stephen accepted a plea bargain and confessed to all the robberies in exchange for a reduction in his sentence to a total of nine years. We had less than two months before he would be formally sentenced and surrender himself to custody. Stephen and I tried to get everything in order, now having some idea what the future would bring.

Wanting to hold onto our home, Stephen worked on projects that needed to be done around the house and even constructed a small apartment for my brother who was planning to move in. My brother needed a place to live, as he was starting a new job, and his contribution would help pay the mortgage. The timing and his presence at the house turned out to be a godsend.

Stephen did some odd jobs for friends and neighbors in the interim, and we sat down together to try to come up with some sort of budget. It was a long shot, but with help from family, and with me working real estate and as a massage therapist, we might be able to keep the boys and me in our home.

As formal sentencing time approached, Stephen asked me the question I had been dreading.

"Will you stay married to me? I know I've done a lot of damage to our relationship, but hopefully not irreparable damage. Come on Jeanne. Can you ever forgive me? You're my wife." He wanted me to wait until he came home again—he promised that he would make it up to all of us. He told me he truly loved the boys and me; he said that was why he had gotten himself into this situation in the first place. It had all been to hold on to us, and after all this, he did not want to lose his family.

I gave him an honest answer. "I don't know Steve." I simply did not know what was ahead for us.

When Stephen asked me to stay with him, I thought to myself, *Why? And how?* I couldn't trust him anymore. I couldn't imagine how a marriage could possibly work when there was no more trust. I didn't admire Stephen anymore. I wanted to be in love with my partner. There had been so many lies from him, too many. The boys and I would suffer for a long time because of all of his mistakes.

Stephen and I had some long discussions as his time at home grew to a close, and there were many tears between us. Often we stayed up all night long and talked about how sad and crazy this whole thing was. How had we spiraled down to this? What had happened to our friendship? We used to be best friends. We used to tell each other everything. We laughed, truly enjoyed each other's company, and respected each other's opinions. Look where we were now. We knew we were both deeply troubled and prayed to God for guidance and peace.

Yet, although we had candid and open conversations now and then about the reality of what had happened, the majority of the time, Stephen tried to go on as if everything was completely normal. He even returned to coaching Little League—but only for a short while. I always forced myself to go to my son's baseball games; I wanted to be there for him. I sat there on the bleachers looking straight ahead, with my oversized sunglasses covering much of my face. I could feel the tension in the stands as I watched my son and Stephen out on the field. It became clear that the parents wanted Stephen to resign from his coaching duties. Finally one of the parents came right up to me in the bleachers and angrily asked, "Why is he still coaching?" I didn't know how to respond.

Stephen was upset by that, but they were right and I understood. Everyone had been very supportive and generous with our family, but a man who had been convicted of robbing banks and had not yet even gone to prison to make his restitution was probably not a good role model for the boys on the team. Stephen couldn't see the other parents' perspective at all; he was very much in denial about a lot of things. He thought he should just be able to coach, and he didn't see why or how it was so disturbing to anyone.

I felt great sorrow over Stephen's plight but was even more upset about how he seemed to want to just put the past behind us as quickly as possible. He had done a lot of damage to the boys and me, and to everyone who knew him and trusted him. His refusal to accept that reality distanced me from him even more, and I lost even more respect for him. He went around town acting as if nothing had happened. I, on the hand, was still struggling with the shame I felt and limited my trips to town to only when it was necessary.

I started to think Stephen was having some sort of a mental breakdown. How else could his denial and assuming behavior be rationalized? It was difficult to keep myself strong and rational for the boys on a day-to-day basis during this time, knowing that I could not come to grips with my own emotions. I did not want to complicate their confusion and sadness with my own sadness and anger—especially when I knew that we were about to have the inevitable conversation with them about Stephen's future.

Stephen and I had to explain to the boys that Daddy was going away for a long time, and not just going away, but going to prison. The boys wanted to know what had happened. What could he have done that was so bad that he'd have to go to jail? We told them that Daddy took money off the counter. We said he had to go away for a long time, but we never said exactly how long. I was told by their therapist not to give them an exact number of years; it would be too much for them to handle all at once. They also wanted to know when they could go visit Daddy and how many times they would be allowed to visit him. They asked if people at school knew, and I explained that the parents did but that the other kids did not know.

The boys loved their dad, and they knew he loved them, too. He had always been a great father. Even when Stephen was at his lowest before his sentencing, he made a point of making sure the boys never suspected how severe the situation was. They didn't really understand what prison was all about, nor did we know anyone who had ever gone to prison. It was very difficult for me to explain in a calm and even manner and to control my resentment toward Stephen. My emotions were all over the place.

The date was finally set. Stephen would be formally sentenced on May 2, 2004, and then start his prison term immediately. When Stephen came home and told me, I burst into tears, seeing his face and thinking about the boys and their pain. At the same time, there was a lot of relief once a date had been set. It was going to be over with, and getting him out of the house at this point was very important for my health. It had been all about Stephen for so long, and the anticipation of him going away had created a lot of anxiety for everyone.

Stephen's preparation for going to prison was literally to pack away his things—things he would not see again for nine years—and get ready to report to custody with only the clothes on his back. He resented me for asking him to pack all of his clothes from the closet and then bring them to his father's house. He wanted to keep his things at our house; he thought he should be able to come back. He finally did it over the last week he was home, but begrudgingly.

Stephen asked me again, on that final day at our home, if I would wait for him while he was in prison.

"Will you remain my wife?"

My thinking and all my attention was centered on my boys and how we would manage to get through the next few days—even the next few hours—not what I was going to do with my future. Again, I told Stephen that I just didn't know.

Because of the media presence, he spent his last night at his father's house. It was the house he grew up in and the house his father would sell a few years later while Stephen was in prison. None of the talks Stephen and I had with the boys during the previous months prepared us for his departure and the final good-bye. As he left to go over to his father's house, it was a heart-wrenching scene. I watched my sons cling to their father's legs. I will never forget the sights and sounds of that pivotal moment in all of our lives.

My three-year-old looked up at him and said, "Wherever you're going, can I come? Please, can I come?"

Our older son, Stephen Jr., then seven, took it the hardest, as he was old enough to understand.

"Please, Daddy, don't leave us, please don't go. Please, please, please," he wailed.

The boys just would not let go of Stephen and kept begging him to stay. They were crying, I was crying, Stephen was crying.

To watch my sons and my husband in so much pain was unbearable. Until that day, I had never really known what it meant when someone would say that their heart had been *broken*. It was then that I understood. I could actually feel the pain in my chest as my own heart broke into pieces.

The boys hugged Stephen all the way to the front door. I sat there on the couch and cried a deep, deep flood of tears, the type of tears I have never experienced before. It was devastating.

Then Stephen left. The door shut behind him.

The boys ran to the window for one last wave before falling into my arms. The three of us continued to sob, and we stayed there on the couch hugging each other for a long, long time. I promised that everything would be okay. Mommy would make everything okay.

The next morning, on the day of Stephen's sentencing, I was in court, waiting in the back with my mother, trying to keep my composure. *Thank God my mother is here,* I thought. My mother is such a private person. It wasn't easy for her to be there because she knew that cameras and the media would be all over the place and that she would very likely be seen on the news that night. I knew it was tough for her to be there, but she is also strong, and I knew she was doing it for me.

As expected, the media was there with cameras right in the courtroom, and I felt them keeping us under constant observation. We watched Stephen as he stepped up to the judge's bench. I was stunned as I saw the man who I had always looked up to for strength now hanging his head in defeat. The courtroom was silent as we all listened to the judge. My mother reached for my hand and held it.

"Stephen Trantel, you had everything and you threw it all away. You have ruined your life," said the judge as he banged down the gavel. I could barely catch my breath, and I felt my eyes fill up with tears. Somehow,

I fixed my stare straight ahead, as I saw Stephen being led out of the courtroom. He turned back to me with a very scared and pathetic look on his face that sent chills up my spine. At this point, the reality hit me. The wonderful life we once had no longer existed. Stephen was on his way to prison. For a very long time.

Stephen's attorney came over and tried to leave us with some kind, hopeful words, but I have no recollection of what he said. My mom and I sat for a while, stunned. We knew there were more reporters waiting outside and hoped that if we stayed in the courtroom long enough, that they would give up and leave.

However, that was not the case. The media was relentless. We waited for over a half an hour. When we finally walked out, there were about eight cameras and a large group of reporters all asking for a statement.

I didn't speak; instead, I hid. But now I wish I had prepared something to read. I wanted to apologize on Stephen's behalf. I wanted to apologize to the banks. I also wish I had the courage at the time to publicly apologize to the bank tellers that he had scared; I realized he may have changed those people's lives forever. I wanted to say sorry to all of his friends and family whom he had disappointed. I wanted to say I was sorry that we had used all that stolen money to pay our bills, but I was paralyzed. No words would come out. It was so hard to be in so much pain, let alone to be in that much pain in front of the cameras.

I just kept looking straight ahead, beyond the reporters, not letting them see me cry. I was determined not to let them see the devastation that was inside of me and inside of everyone who knew Stephen. It was a sad day for Stephen's family and all his friends. Who would ever think that things would turn out like this? Never could I have imagined my husband, Stephen, committing any type of crime—let alone a crime that would land him in prison for the next nine years.

I went back to our home. There I was, alone with my boys, consumed by a wild mixture of raw emotions. Stephen had left us; he had left me to pick up the pieces.

CHAPTER NINE
PICKING UP THE PIECES

It was early May. Like most Long Islanders, this had always been the time of year I looked forward to with eager anticipation. I loved the warm, sunny weather and spending time at the beach. However, even the approaching summer could not break through the heavy feeling of dread I carried around with me. Stephen had just started his prison term. I couldn't sleep and spent my nights pacing around my bedroom. I was completely lost and woke up every day with a terrible sinking feeling inside of me. It was a feeling of doom. Questions consumed me: What was I going to do? How was I going to take care of myself and the boys? What if I wasn't able to find a job? How was I going to do it all without Stephen? I was overwhelmed and thought I was not going to make it. I felt I couldn't go on.

As heavy and demanding as everything during that

time felt, in many ways I also felt relieved to have Stephen finally out of the house. I started to feel a certain freedom I hadn't felt in a long time. There was a part of me that celebrated being separated from him and the fact that all that I had to endure while he was out on bail those six months was finally over with. It was all about Stephen for so long—everything had revolved around his sentencing, and his friends had encouraged the victim role he was playing by feeling so sorry for him. His friends believed he *had* to rob the banks and that he did it because of me—and for me. I was tired of the accusations coming my way instead of toward Stephen. How had I become the bad guy? I got tired of explaining over and over again how I had always been more than willing to work, but that Stephen had insisted I stay home with the boys, promising there was no need for me to supplement our income. Stephen had been really angry with me those six months he was home and took out all his frustrations on me. He played the victim, and I was glad not to have to take the brunt of his moods and attitude any longer.

With Stephen gone, there was much to do between taking care of the boys, going to school full-time, and going to my real estate job. I wanted to be the best mom I could possibly be and provide the kids with as much of a normal life as possible. I was thinking too much, probably over-thinking everything. Once Stephen was in prison, I discovered a few other nasty little secrets. Stephen had taken out a credit card in my name and there was suddenly a $5,000 debt I had to pay back. When I asked him about it he gave me his usual defense.

"Jeanne I did it for us."

Picking up the pieces of my life was the hardest thing I've ever done. Suddenly, I was forced to confront the outside world after years of remaining somewhat cocooned in my home. It helped to have my twin brother Richard move in to help with the mortgage and the boys. His sense of humor made the days and evenings go by a little easier. I was suddenly a single mother and going to school full-time. Going to back to work was frightening to me. It had been so long since I'd earned my own money I wasn't confident in my ability to do so any longer.

I read *The Power of Now* by Eckhart Tolle which was recommended to me by a friend. That was the first step in a long journey of steps. The book gave me a glimpse of being present in the power of the current moment. I started to heal with that book. I began to realize that I couldn't dwell on the past, I had to deal with now, this moment. I would have to find the strength inside of myself to move forward.

My days were always filled with anxiety, but I did my best not to show it. I would bring Ryan, my three-year-old, to school with me some days if I did not have the proper childcare. The teachers were very kind to allow me to do that. The students were very understanding and accommodating as well. I also often brought Ryan with me when I went to my real estate office to work. Each day, I simply did what was necessary to get through the day and make things work the best I could.

"Here, draw Mommy a picture," I'd say, setting Ryan up with a paper and crayons near my desk.

Amazingly, the principal of Ryan's preschool let Ryan stay in school for a year for free. When she told me that I wouldn't have to pull him out of school and away from the friends he'd made there, I cried.

My last experience with the media at the time of Stephen's sentencing had taken its toll on me. A picture of me leaving court had appeared in a New York newspaper. That article and other articles like it were very hurtful and demeaning. My first weeks at home without Stephen left me paranoid once again. I was worried about being followed by the media, and I was worried about the boys and what they might be subjected to when they went back to school or were at any of their social or athletic activities. Most people were kind, but I was always nervous about it. I wanted to keep them sheltered from any hurtfulness, either intentional or unintentional.

Stephen started serving his nine-year sentence at the Nassau County jail, awaiting transfer upstate to a maximum-security prison. Visiting him there was reliving the same nightmare as when he was first arrested. A part of me felt sorry for him, but another part of me felt like he deserved it. When I visited, I could not wait to leave. Seeing him did not ease my pain, it only intensified it. Stephen had always been a man of confidence, but that trait was now missing from his persona. I no longer recognized Stephen as the man I married—there was so little trace of the man I once knew. He looked thin, frail, and completely helpless; not knowing what the next prison would be like and how he would make it through his nine-year sentence was clearly weighing on him. Though I was not the one in prison, in a strange way, I felt imprisoned by my emotions and my lack of energy for life. I was sharing his time with him.

I got up every morning and prepared the boys for school, trying to get things back to normal for our family. But as soon as they were gone and I was alone again, I often went back to grieving. My mother and my friends visited every day to offer encouragement and tried to get me out of the house more often. I appreciated all their efforts, and I made an effort to be polite and amenable to their suggestions, but it was difficult. I really just wanted to be left alone, alone with my sorrow. It was strange because the minute I was alone, I wanted and needed company.

It seemed every time I turned around, it was one step forward, then two steps backward. One day, a girlfriend came over to help me organize and pack up Stephen's belongings. He had taken his clothes to his father's house as I had requested, but there was still so much of Stephen's life in our home. It was very sad, like someone had died, but it had to be done and we both shed many tears during the process. My therapist pointed out that in order to truly move forward, I needed to clear our home of memories from the past that kept the pain alive and prevented me from healing. It was very hard to see all the old pictures of me and Stephen as a couple; it didn't help me move forward, it only took me steps back. It was important to take those down. I kept pictures of him with the kids and put those photos in their room. I did not want to be reminded of Stephen every time I turned around, so I made the decision to clean out and start fresh.

My friend and I were just finishing up inside the house and were moving some boxes into the garage when I came upon a plastic bag stuffed in the corner. I pulled the bag out, reached inside, and was stunned by what I found.

"Oh my God!" I shrieked and threw the bag and its contents onto the floor.

My girlfriend ran to me and screamed, "Oh my God, what is it?"

We both just stared in astonishment. There at my feet was one of the disguises Stephen had worn during a bank robbery—a wig and a pair of black rimmed sunglasses. I said not a word. I didn't have to. She understood. I was shaking and felt myself coming undone. I turned around, walked out of the garage, and went back to the shelter of my bedroom where I sat and wept.

Still, there were blessings that appeared out of nowhere during that time. I knew I had an amazing support group, and I realize now that my family and friends all pitched in and helped pick up the shattered pieces around me. Pieces that I could not even see at the time. They understood there were so many things I just could not face and instinctively did whatever they could to help.

"What if we don't make it?" I asked my brother Robert more than once.

"You'll make it," he always assured me. "You're not alone."

Anonymous gifts of money appeared, as well as more gift cards and coupons for groceries. People continued to cook for us, and others invited the boys over to play with their children or join them for special events and outings. My brother had moved in and was contributing toward the mortgage, and with help from my parents, the financial burden had temporarily eased. I was surrounded by so much love and support and I had to keep going through the motions for the boys. I cooked, cleaned, did laundry, and helped the boys with their homework, but I really did not focus on what I was doing or do it with much care. I could not see a future before me, and I had only enough energy to accomplish the bare minimum. I was half-heartedly setting myself up to start selling real estate full time now that the boys were in school. I was attending massage school, even stepping up my hours. My father had paid for me to go to school and I didn't want to disappoint him. I knew I had to complete my schooling as quickly as possible so that I could begin bringing in a real income. In the meantime, I babysat for neighbors and did what I could to bring in some extra cash.

It was a beautiful, sunny, Long Island summer, but I continued to walk in darkness and despair for a long, long time.

In August, Stephen was transferred to Downstate Correctional Facility, a maximum-security prison. Despite my pain and depression, I was determined that our children would continue to have a relationship with their father. Although some people thought the boys should be sheltered from the prison experience, I believed they should visit Stephen. As difficult as the circumstances were, Stephen needed his boys and they needed him. From the boys' perspective, they simply loved their father and wanted to see him, no matter where he was. From my perspective, in relationship to Stephen and me as a couple, I realized that the situation was beyond our control now. This was a very profound and decisive realization for me. We were both on our own. To survive—or not. Although visiting Stephen was a terrible ordeal for me, I drew great strength from seeing my boys' innocence and their devotion to their father. It was amazing to see that kind of love in its purest form. That is why I knew that taking the boys to such a dreadful environment, even at their young ages, was the right thing to do.

It was a two-hour drive from our home to the state prison. The facility was terrible, covered in barbed wire, just like in the movies. The boys and I would wait in line to be moved through metal detectors and then led to a large room where we would visit with Stephen. The room was a sea of men in green prison uniforms with guards every five feet. The environment was as bleak as was the future of most of the men incarcerated there. The despair and poverty of many of the visitors was quite apparent too.

During one visit, we shared the same table as two young men who, I found out, were brothers. When I asked Stephen what they were in for, he told me that they were serving life sentences for murdering their parents. As I sat there, I felt myself almost lifting out of my body in disbelief. I wondered what terrible things the other men around us had done to get there and felt the fear choking in my throat as I struggled to stay strong for the boys. It was as if I were in a movie; I was an actress playing the role of the dutiful wife visiting her innocent husband in prison. However, the fact was that Stephen was not innocent and this was no movie. It was my life. And, it was very different from the perfect life I once thought I had.

Our visits usually lasted a few hours, which was a long time for small boys to be occupied in a confined space. Stephen Jr. and Ryan crawled all over Stephen, unable to stop touching him.

"Look Daddy!" Ryan would yell, trying to get all of Stephen's attention.

"Do you like it here?" Stephen Jr. asked. Stephen was clear that he didn't like it where he was and couldn't wait to come home to be with them. He lit up when the boys filled him in on softball and school and their friends. When visiting hours were over, I was more than ready to leave, but it was always a gut-wrenching good-bye. Leaving Stephen in a place like that was still somehow unimaginable to me. The boys and I would make the drive home, with me crying as they sat in the backseat, saying not a word.

I brought the kids to visit Stephen about once every eight weeks, but the family also helped out because I was always working or going to school, including some Saturday courses. Stephen and I were very distant from each other during those visits; it was all about the kids. That's where we kept the focus. I still had a lot of anger and other feelings that I was working out. I was also working on forgiving Stephen, but I have found that these things take a lot of time. It is a process and certainly did not happen overnight for me. There was so much devastation; he had put the family through destruction at its finest. I would always bring him money and food, but only because I believed that was the right thing to do as a human being.

Before long, though, I grew tired of being the dutiful wife, even for the sake of my sons. I began to feel the rage everyone had been telling me I would eventually feel. My grief had turned to fiery anger and hate. I became enraged with Stephen. For seven years, I had been a stay-at-home mom, content to tend to the boys' needs while Stephen was the breadwinner. It was what we both had wanted. But, when things got tough, Stephen hadn't been honest with me. He had not trusted me and never gave us a chance to work together to figure things out. How dare Stephen take such control of our lives and then destroy them?

This was another dark, dark time in my life. For me, that period turned out to be my time of mourning. I was grieving. I was grieving the loss of my husband and our once happy life. I was spiraling downward even further and knew it, but I did not care. In a way I hit rock bottom emotionally.

I was very angry about what he had done, but more than anything, it was his cavalier and nonchalant attitude that really infuriated me. It seemed that all he wanted to do was put everything in the past. He never addressed the reality of what he had done, the pain and destruction he had caused, or what he left in the wake of his choices. He didn't admit to the magnitude of his actions or the consequences those actions imposed on everyone close to him. He put blinders on and refused to see things as they really were and take full responsibility for his actions. What sort of example was that for him to set for our children?

I also had a hard time not being furious about the fact that he thought I should stay in the marriage. He sensed that I was pulling further and further away from him.

"For better or worse," he reminded me, not leaving room to discuss the possibility. In his tone, there was a smugness that I found offensive. His parents had been together until his mother's death and he knew how upsetting my parents' divorce had been for me.

I always answered, "You left me the day you robbed the first bank." And hadn't he? What did he think was going to happen? Did he actually think that he'd get away with it? And how could he make me a part of something so ugly? It infuriated me that he chose to take care of his family by robbing banks. And yet, I felt strangely helpless.

As happens with the ebb and flow of the strong emotions we experience in life, there finally came a day when I felt a glimmer of strength deep within. Though it was a result of the fiery anger I had been feeling, it somehow also broke through the barrier or that anger. The shift took place when I was sitting in my room, crying and crying. It was the middle of the night. My inner conscious started to nag at me. My sons needed me. I had no alternative; I needed to become a stronger person and take control of my life. The sorrow had turned to anger, and, it was the anger that first motivated me, but the anger had shifted.

All of a sudden, I came to the realization that I had to stop blaming Stephen for my life as it was now. I had to move on and start a new life. I had to take responsibility for my own pain and get happy with myself. I realized that I wanted to change my life so badly, I was willing to do whatever it took. I felt a huge drive to succeed inside—even if the drive was simply the result of having no choice but to succeed.

I knew I had to change and that I had to dig more inside myself. I realized that I needed to become more empowered and take back the reins. I had to step more into my life—with more purpose and determination. During this entire turning point in my room that night, I could actually feel the change happening inside me.

I slowly got myself up and going again. Stepping back into my old world was not easy, but it wasn't really my old world after all. Things had changed, my role had changed, and I didn't know where I fit in. I knew I had no choice but to build a new world and a new life for us as a family of three.

I threw myself full force into real estate. I was determined to balance the boys, work, and home. I just kept going through the motions—day after day—trying to do the right thing. I am not sure if it was luck, skill, or pure determination, but I was successful in getting listings and selling houses immediately. I had closings and thankfully started producing income right away. In my first year, I sold a 2.3 million dollar home, and that commission paid my mortgage for eight months. My confidence was building. I began to feel a little bit better about myself and more hopeful that there was a future out there for my boys and me. It was empowering for me to open a personal bank account.

It felt better than the first time I'd opened one when I was a teenager. Now I was a woman with two children and this money was going to be used to support our family.

I was still bitter about losing my old life. Not the money or the cars or the vacations. To me my old life was a life of blissful ignorance. However, I finally realized it was not doing anyone any good to hate Stephen and to hang on to so much negativity. With the help of a combination of therapy, reading, and soul searching, I began the process of letting go of my dependency on Stephen and finding my own freedom.

Months earlier, several people had said, "Aren't you furious with Stephen? You have to leave him!" Back then, that was the furthest thing from my mind, and I was angry with anyone who suggested that to me.

At that time, I believe that I still loved my husband. How could I desert him as he was headed to prison? But many things had changed in my heart and soul since those conversations, and there came a time when I felt that I had stood behind Stephen long enough. I decided it was time to divorce.

It took me a year to actually divorce Stephen after my initial impulse. I prayed on it. I went to a priest. Stephen didn't believe in divorce and neither did I; I remembered all too keenly what my parents' divorce had done to me. I didn't want that for my children. I felt a large amount of guilt; how could I leave him at the lowest point in his life? Marriage was supposed to be for life. But I wasn't in love with him anymore. The priest I spoke with told me that I had to do what I felt was right. He told me that I could be a support to Stephen, as the father of my children, without being married to him.

The time between Stephen's arrest in November and the start of his prison sentence the following May had taken a fatal toll on our marriage. Stephen had become a stranger to me in so many ways. I was not happy with the way he treated me during those most difficult months. I could not condone what he had done, no matter what his rationalization had been, and there had been too much deception. I had lost respect for Stephen as a person, and I harbored a great deal of doubt about him—and about us. As I told him in that one moment of strength, it became clear that Stephen stopped being true to me and to our marriage the day he robbed the first bank.

It was a painful step for me, but a divorce was the only way to really start all over again.

Stephen was going to spend the next nine years in

prison, and I felt that I needed to move on without him. I knew I would not be there waiting for Stephen as his wife when he finished serving his sentence and it wasn't fair to either one of us to pretend that I would be. He needed to know that. I did not divorce Stephen because he was in prison or because of the length of his term. Although I knew I didn't want to put my life on hold and wait for him, the ultimate reason for my decision was that I realized we were no longer friends—and without the friendship, there was no love.

What sparked my decision was also the awareness that I didn't deserve this kind of life he had dropped us into. I had never asked for any of it, and neither had the boys. He could not be the husband I loved or admired anymore; he had changed. I thought about the time I had gone to visit him in jail, when I was waiting in line and then was thrown against the lockers and screamed at to move. There was so much commotion, and it was so traumatic; yet, when I saw Stephen, he just wanted my help. He made no attempt to comfort me or help me. He said he needed me to do this and that and gave me a list of things he wanted me to bring for him on my next visit. He went on to tell me that the other inmates were bothering him and complained about the conditions there, trying to get me to feel his pain.

I was not going to go down his dark road anymore.

When I approached Stephen and let him know I wanted a divorce, he was very angry. He made me feel guilty, saying again that he thought marriage was "for better or for worse" and tried to persuade me not to divorce him. I told him I had made my decision; my love for him was no longer there. I made it clear to him that he couldn't give me what I needed. I didn't need a big house and expensive cars, jewelry and clothes. I needed a friend and a lover. I needed someone that my boys could respect and look up to. I wanted a better life for the boys and for me. I vowed to work toward keeping a friendship between us and to do all I could to help maintain his relationship with his sons.

Though Stephen was wounded and very upset with me, eventually he seemed to accept this. During the process of our divorce, our relationship became more adversarial and sometimes even combative, but for the sake of the boys, we knew that ultimately we had to resolve our feelings for each other. The divorce, though it was through my insistence, was another heartbreak for me. I had always believed that Stephen and I would be together for the rest of our lives. All my dreams had been shattered, but I resolved to start over.

CHAPTER TEN
STARTING OVER

That sinking feeling when I awoke in the morning lasted a very long time—for at least three years. It was not every day, and has diminished over time, but it was often enough to be unhealthy. My pain was so deep; it felt like my soul was just giving up. Intellectually, I recognized that I had to overcome this state of mind. Just trying to survive is not the way to live your life. I knew that life should be lived with contentment in your heart and soul, no matter what your circumstances. I turned to God and asked him for strength and the ability to forgive. Slowly my prayers began to be answered.

Outwardly, I tried to do all the right things for the boys and for myself. I was worried about their happiness, and the last thing I wanted to have happen was to have their childhoods stolen from them. We were able to remain in the house and neighborhood where so many wonderful people surrounded us. It was very important to me that the boys be in a stable environment. Through much love and compassion, they have thrived at their neighborhood school and in our community.

One day I was in the car with my son Stephen Jr. and he said, "You know, if this with daddy hadn't happened you wouldn't be the strong person that you are." And he was so right.

My relationship with Stephen has gotten better through the years, although he has never quite gotten over the fact that I divorced him. He believes that I gave up on him. He refuses to recognize the fact that he gave up on me by keeping me in the dark for so long. He also gave up on himself. I am still sometimes resentful toward him for what he did, but I try to be compassionate towards him. His journey is his journey and my journey is mine. In so many ways, whether it is emotionally or financially, I am still working to undo his mistakes. It has been difficult, but I continue to strive to keep the bond between the boys and their dad. Stephen calls every Wednesday night, and the boys visit at least every eight weeks.

Stephen's sister and cousin bring the boys to the

prison most of the time now. They have been a huge part of keeping the boys and their dad close, and I am very grateful for that. I go only occasionally. At a certain point I felt it was time for me to step away and for the boys to have their own relationship with Stephen—one that did not include me.

The prison has a fantastic visitation program. The boys can have overnight visits with their dad in a cabin on the prison grounds. The visitation program is for two nights, and Stephen's sister goes with them to sleep over as well. Since I am no longer Stephen's wife, I am not allowed to participate. It was very hard at first to feel comfortable with my children staying on the prison grounds, but it has turned out to be a wonderful experience for them. Those weekends have given the boys special time with their dad. Never would I have thought that one day my two precious children would be going to a prison for a mini-vacation. Very different from our weekends in Montauk, but one never knows what twists and turns life has in store for us. As in any situation in life, you make the most of it and do the best thing for everyone concerned. I understand that it is not just about me and my feelings. I have learned to be much more objective.

The boys and I went to counseling. They have

changed, but they have changed in a beautiful way. In the beginning, it was very hard, but we all have gotten used to our new life. The boys are angry sometimes as they feel the loss of their father, but we talk about it and love prevails. They know that they are loved and that there will be a time when they will have a father in their daily lives, even if that time is not for a few more years. I tell my sons that they have taught me so much about unconditional love and that they are great examples for me to follow. I am very proud of them.

"Hats off," I always say, "Hats off to my two boys."

I knew it was important to set my sights on financial independence, and so I became something I did not think possible—a single mom and a career woman. In my first year as a real estate agent, I was a very high producer. I worked hard and it gave me a great sense of accomplishment. I am constantly balancing my work schedule so that I can be with the boys as much as possible when they are not at school. Things get very hectic, but I see that as one of the joys of being a working mother.

A real estate career has its highs and lows, so my income was variable and—not surprisingly—I continued to have many setbacks with paying my bills.

I am not unlike a lot of people in a difficult economy. But, I was proud to actually go through the action of paying a bill. Each bill payment felt like a victory for me – financially and emotionally. I graduated from massage school and took on clients at the local gym and country club. Even working the two jobs, I still required financial assistance from my dad. He has been very generous to us and has given me a big jumpstart in life. It humbles me to have to accept my father's help, but not necessarily in a bad way. Stephen couldn't ask for help and ended up in prison.

My father has been a blessing in our lives in so many ways. He has been an amazing influence on my boys. My dad was a great dad, and now he is a wonderful grandfather. He always had lots of time for his children, and he is the same with his grandchildren. He is always stopping in to check on us, and he helps me with the boys most weekends, as that is my busiest time selling real estate. It is a very good feeling for a mom to know she is leaving her children with such a caring and loving man.

My mom has been a great help with the boys as well. She is a fabulous mother and grandmother, or "Mimi" as my boys call her. She helps with what I call many of the "extras" for the boys. She has paid for their tutors, shopped for new clothes for them, and helped in so many other ways.

"I'm going to take Ryan to buy a new pair of pants," she'll say, or, "What shoe size is Stevie now?"

My brothers are always coming over to play baseball with the boys and are remarkable role models. Family is so important, and I am so very grateful for mine. I know I could not have made this healing journey without them.

Every day continues to be a struggle for me financially, but I am sure that that is the case with many single parents. I lived without health insurance for four years, as I could not afford it for a long time. I finally got medical assistance for the boys through a state program for children under the age of eighteen. I now have private health insurance for myself. It is costly, but a necessity.

As far as the debt incurred in the last years of our marriage, Stephen will be required to pay restitution for the stolen money. In the meantime, it has taken me years to clear up loans, credit card balances, and legal fees. I do know in my heart that the struggle is worth it. The joy and love that the boys and I share is a wonderful gift.

Although on some level I understood early on

that I needed to work toward releasing myself from the disappointment and anger that had turned into terrible hate, it has been a long road. I have traveled that arduous road to what I call "enlightenment." I had always believed in God and had strong religious convictions as a Catholic. However, once Stephen went to jail, I was forced to do a lot of soul-searching. I have a very powerful faith in Jesus and Mother Mary, and I go to St. Paul's Cathedral, a beautiful church in Hempstead, a neighboring town, where there is a tearing icon. Many miracles happen at this church, and the church brings much peace to those who go to pray there. I have done a lot of praying there myself; it is a place where I find myself closer to God.

I have a great friend who is a life coach. Without charging me a cent she helped me through some very tough times.

I discovered that attending workshops and meeting new people who were also on journeys of their own gave me great comfort and insight.

One such forum was a four-day session about turning an ordinary life into an extraordinary life, and it was fabulous. This was an introduction to Ramtha's School of Enlightenment where you learn about the biology of the brain, how to create reality and really live your dreams based on making known the unknown. Ramtha's School of Enlightenment is the original school of consciousness and energy, using ancient wisdom and the latest discoveries of neuroscience and quantum physics to help people access the extraordinary abilities of their brain and live a remarkable life. JZ Knight is the founder of the school. She is also the channel for Ramtha, the enlightened one. Peace came to me after that class. I experienced a calmness I had never felt before. I am continuing to attend classes offered at the school in order to further develop my remarkable life. I also studied online through classes with Oprah Winfrey and Eckhart Tolle on Monday nights, examining a book called *New Earth*.

I am always striving for new ways to better myself. I continually do self-help workshops when my budget allows, and I do a great deal of reading in the interim. Books by Marianne Williamson and Wayne Dyer were life changing for me. I have learned so much about others and myself through these programs. I believe I am a more open-minded and loving person because of them. I know my studies have played a huge role in helping me heal. Once I had to let go of the material comforts that came with being married to Stephen, I was able to discover and nurture spiritual comforts.

Socially, my world has changed. I still have all my childhood friends, but understandably, I am not as close as I used to be with many of the friends Stephen and I had as a couple. Couples seem to do things with other couples, and it was no fun for me to be the odd man, or rather, woman out. In suburbia, you definitely have a different social life as a single mom than you did when you were part of a couple. However, although I am different from those around me, I am still quite close to all my girlfriends; no one deserted me. I also made new friends through my work and spiritual studies. My social circle now includes a diverse cross section of people of all ages and from all lifestyles.

For a long time, my heart was not in it, but eventually I started to date. I am sure my dating stories are similar to most others, but I've had my share of catastrophes. It is always the small talk in the beginning that makes me feel uncomfortable. It is difficult to avoid the all too familiar questions, "Why did you and your husband split up?" or "Where is your ex-husband now?" You can imagine the uneasiness I encounter when a man hears even part of my story. It is not a good subject to bring up on a first date, but there is no getting around the truth.

I remember going on a dinner date, and the man

asking about my ex-husband. When I told him, his mouth dropped. We ate quickly, he drove me home very fast, and that was the last time I heard from him. Oh well! Finding the time to date with all the kids' activities and working is not easy. However, my boys are my top priority. I hope that the time will come when I find the right person and I will remarry. I believe in the values of marriage and know the importance of open communication, no matter what the circumstances and how hard it may be to tell the truth. Above all, there must be a great friendship, respect, and trust.

Through it all, I knew a priority for me was to take care of my physical health. I go to the gym regularly and take a variety of classes. My local gym, Sky Athletic Club, is a wonderful gym. It turns out that the gym has been a great place for me professionally and socially as well. I have made connections for massage clients and real estate customers while meeting many new friends there. I still love being outdoors, and when the weather and my schedule permit, I head to the beach for long walks and times of solace.

I work on every area of my life to try to pull things together. It is hard work, exhausting even, and I have many setbacks along the way. Even with all my setbacks and disappointments though, I am continually blessed by the love and support surrounding me. Although it is painful, I dig deep inside of myself to find the answers. They are there, in my soul, and that is where I find hope and my vision for a better future.

People ask me all the time, "How could you not know what your husband was doing?" My answer is always the same: "Why would I think that? Who would ever think that?" No one who knew Stephen had any reason for such a thought about him to even cross their mind; that's why it was such a shock to everyone—including me.

Why would I, a woman who was married to her husband for ten years, who had been with him for twelve years, imagine that he was robbing banks? He was a Wall Street trader, a Little League coach. He was always the upright man. No one would have believed that of him.

I was the one closest to him, but I had my head in the sand. I gave my husband my power. Stephen worked, and I took care of the kids. He had his role, I had mine, and we loved it. It worked for us, but only for awhile. When things got tough, Stephen, my husband and best friend, did not come to me, as his partner, to help figure things out. I so regret that. But I didn't rob those banks. He did.

One of the biggest things that I've had to heal from is my own guilt and shame. For a long time I felt like a *fool*. Stephen had made a fool of me, and I had also made a fool of myself. I had been blissfully ignorant for years, buried in the cocoon of married life. Play dates and dinner kept me from seeing what was really going on in my marriage. I had allowed someone else to control my life by controlling my finances and eventually my feelings. I had put the lives of my children in jeopardy because of not insisting on becoming involved. I hadn't had a personal bank account for years. I was content with the wads of cash given to me by my husband and promises.

For so many years, I had simply been Stephen's wife. I did what he told me to and I didn't ask questions. I hadn't realized how passive I was. I felt as much a victim as Stephen's crimes as the people whose money that he robbed. I needed to move beyond allowing myself to be victimized, and then demonized. Stephen told me that he had done it for me and the boys which made me out to be the selfish trophy wife. I knew that I wasn't this person that Stephen had decided I was; yet, I still wasn't sure who I was.

Reclaiming my life has been a process. I took a hard look at myself to understand my weaknesses and my role in what happened. Recovering and trying to move forward is not enough. I learned that accepting responsibility and examining one's thought patterns, instilled beliefs, and habits is a critical part of any recovery. In order to truly heal, I needed to do a lot of soul-searching. And I did.

CHAPTER ELEVEN
Now

If I have one thing to say to other women, it is this: "Be involved with your household finances." I realized I had allowed my husband to control our financial lives. We lived our lives with the optimism that our income would always be there and always improve. The old adage of "saving for a rainy day" is so true, but perhaps that saying ought to be "saving for a rainy year." I should have made it a point to be familiar with what our expenses were; if I had done that, we could have budgeted better and done it together. If I had been more aware of how much money it took to run our home, I would have known we were in trouble. It would have been a shared problem, not one that Stephen felt he needed to resolve himself. It would have saved me, Stephen, my children and the rest of my family a lot of grief.

Stephen could not handle our financial crisis, and he was not as invincible as I thought he was. I have come to realize that Stephen was not confident or trusting enough in my abilities to ask for help when necessary and to come up with solutions. Part of that is my responsibility. I didn't want to see problems and was too dependent on him. I expected him to take care of me and had to learn how to take care of myself.

I urge others not to make the same mistakes. Show interest and be proactive. Be a partner in your current finances, and do whatever you can to help plan your financial future.

I am more careful now. I have to watch every penny. I budget to make my income stretch month to month. My real estate income is variable as I only earn income when I have a successful sale. That often means working many hours, days, or weeks with no return, and sometimes waiting sixty to ninety days for compensation when I do finally get a house in contract. My bookings for massage therapy can be sporadic as well, so I have to keep my schedule flexible and always be ready to work as the opportunity arises. The financial responsibility for my family has made me much wiser and more attentive.

I am awake now. My eyes are wide open. And I will

never stick my head in the sand again. I've discovered that ignorance is the opposite of bliss.

I feel very rich in a different way now. My richness comes from a great family and many friends. It is not how much money you have in the bank that is important, especially since that can be stolen; it is how much love you have within and around you. This is a point that I emphasize with my children.

I was in a relationship in which I allowed my husband to have too much power over our lives. I willingly gave him that power because it was easier for me. I admit I liked being taken care of. I am still paying for that. In desperation, Stephen turned to crime. Although he rationalized that bank robbery was a victimless crime, he hurt many people along the way. Stephen knew that what he was doing was wrong, and that should have been enough to stop him. But it wasn't. He did not see things clearly or he would have known that the ramifications of his negative actions would extend to his family, his friends, and his community. I do not believe he ever realized how destructive and far-reaching his actions would ultimately be.

Stephen has lost his freedom and is serving his time in prison, but my boys and I have lost a piece of our lives as well. Our extended family and friends were hurt and disappointed, and they feel the hurt for us as well. We can sit, dwell, and be bitter, or we can forgive. Forgiving does not mean we condone or pardon, but it does allow us to move on with a peaceful heart. I forgive him and I forgive myself.

Forgiveness can be a full-time job.

There is no excuse for what Stephen did, but forgiveness is my choice, and one that is well worth making as it gives me freedom from the burden of anger. But, it is never easy. It serves no purpose to hang on to anger and negativity. I believe we are co-creators of our own lives, and when I stopped blaming Stephen, my life started to take a new direction and the healing process began. With faith and love, any achievement is possible, and no matter how much adversity you face, if you dig deep enough, you can find the strength and the answers.

I do believe the boys got a raw deal. I wish they were growing up with a father, but this is the way it is. They did not deserve all this. Yet, although Stephen's robberies tore our family apart, we have managed to put the pieces back together. The boys have become happy and well-adjusted children because they are loved by so many people. Through my family's support and regular therapy, they are thriving. I have learned that you become a very rich person when a great family and friends surround you.

Once I learned the value of forgiveness, I was able to move from anger at Stephen into empowerment. To me, empowerment means the ability to take hold of my life, and to clearly see the loving and giving way to live. I strive to solve problems head on and with a positive attitude, turning those problems into opportunities. Whether it is an opportunity to learn, grow, or improve, I try not to fear obstacles. I want to enjoy each day and not waste one precious moment.

Are we not always a work in progress? I continue to work toward becoming a better, more peaceful person. I am part of a wonderful group of people who meet regularly, and we all are working on our healing. The deeper I go in my spirituality, the easier it gets.

Do I wish my life were different? Not anymore. I am grateful for all that I do have. I have a life that is now filled with blessings. In the beginning, I struggled so hard to resolve my pain simply because I thought I had no choice but to do it—for my children. But, it turns out that I did it for myself; I needed to make this journey for me.

My two children, my boys ... they are pure love. What does it mean to have love, to have pure, unconditional love? The boys constantly show me the way to unconditional love. When we go to the prison, my sons are in the moment. They never judge, and they are not afraid. I used to go in for a visit with Stephen, and I judged. The boys never asked who the inmates were or what they had done, while I always wondered. They did not see race or economic status, even though it was clear that many of the other visiting families were impoverished. They have always only seen their dad. They have lived in the moment of loving him. I feel so grateful to them for the purity of their love and the example they have set for me.

It is easy to love someone when things are good, when there are nice cars, vacations, and a nice house. We all strive for "the perfect life." However, when things get bad or things do not go the way we planned, that is when we are challenged. That is when we learn what we are made of and are able to discover the best in ourselves. We often look for someone to blame, and we become negative and angry. When things are bad is when you must go deep inside yourself to find unconditional love, regardless of your disappointment. It's there. I have learned that from my boys. They easily love, and they easily forgive. I pray that this is a quality they take with them to adulthood and a value they will practice throughout the rest of their lives.

I have gained perspective through my ordeal, not only about my life, but also about the lives of people I have glimpsed along the way. I have a new appreciation for the struggles of the people I've met in prison—not only the inmates, but their loved ones as well, so many of whom are desperate. My problems seem to shrink in comparison to some of the other visitors. Many are very poor people, women mostly, with hungry mouths to feed but without the skills and support needed to get back on their feet. This was a side of life I never would have seen in my sheltered existence. I am a better person because I have seen this other side of life. I am considerate of others who struggle with money, understanding of those who are single parents, and most of all closer to my kids and God. As far as the perfect life goes, we all know there really isn't such a thing. The perfect life can only exist inside your heart and inside of your soul. That is where one should strive for perfection.

I lost at least two crazy years of my life because I was always upset about the past and afraid of the future, but no more. I do not waste my time on small things or the things I have no control over. I have been able to let go of my negative emotions and to live life only in the positive and in the here and now. And most importantly, I always count my blessings! I find myself much more objective about other people and their struggles. It is so true that you should not judge other people unless you have walked in their shoes.

I also believe in a higher power we all have within us, the power I hope to instill in my own children. I have realized that life is all about not missing the moments of here and now, and that it's so important to treat people with respect and integrity every step of the way. When we leave here, we cannot take our homes, our cars, and our possessions; what we take are our souls! The most important thing to me is being with my kids, enjoying them day to day, and loving and appreciating them for who they are. Even when the present moment is painful, and not what we expected, facing the reality of the moment with optimism, hope, and an open mind is the surest way to true happiness.

For all I have been through, I now have a firm belief in the power of visualizing the life you want to live. It can be done. I know, because I did it. I knew I had to be strong. I knew I had to find a way to support the boys and myself, no matter what the obstacles. With the help of my devoted family and friends, I did that. I was lucky. I was blessed and learned that it is all right to take comfort and assistance from those who offer. It is very important to be in the company of people who truly love you for who you are and are a positive influence on you. Be with those who can lift you up when you are down, and those who can lend a hand when you need it. I understand how to be an excellent friend after this experience. I am a better listener, and I have become much more open-minded and loving.

I decided to tell my story, not to gain sympathy for my ex-husband or myself, but because I believe there are others who have been in, or are presently in, similar situations. Many are facing financial and career problems right now and do not know where to turn. So much has changed in our world. Whether it is a family, or an individual, many lives are in crisis. Perhaps my message will give someone the strength to journey to a place in their hearts where they need to be.

It is not my desire to glorify Stephen's character in this book or to destroy it. Stephen has his own story, and he has taken his own painful journey. What happened, happened. It was a terrible mistake in judgment—a decision to go down the wrong path. For me, it would have been easy to allow my anger and bitterness over Stephen's betrayal to ruin my life. In fact, I was on that path for long time. Instead, I have emerged a stronger person, understanding my own frailties and refusing to give in to the toxic effect that negative emotions have on one's life. I finally realized that there is a light at the end of every tunnel and always room for self-improvement.

I hope my words can inspire others who have suffered with internal or external turmoil. I have come to believe that this terrible ordeal had been a blessing in disguise. My story might save even one person from making the kinds of devastating choices that my ex-husband made. Perhaps my message will touch the hearts of women who find themselves in similarly dire circumstances and have felt deep despair as I did. I encourage you to look deep inside and to look to God. Accept the help and love of those who offer it. Things are still difficult for me at times and I still have my struggles, but I know how to find my serenity. Not only can you survive, you can ultimately triumph over difficult—even devastating—circumstances, and live a life filled with blessings. I know it's possible, because I found those blessings. And, for that, I will be ever thankful.

I recognize my own weaknesses and now understand how those flaws may have unwittingly contributed to our family's tragedy. Like Stephen, like everyone, I am a work in progress. Yet, now I know that I will never live my life with my head in the sand ever again. My eyes are opened.

I have struggled these last five years, but because of all I have been through, I emerged a better person. I have known hopelessness and despair, and through my ordeal, have learned that with faith and forgiveness, there are ways to overcome even the biggest and most challenging problems in life. Moving from the emotions of pain and anger to a place of acceptance and peace is a long process—a grieving process—and perhaps my experience can help others face and overcome their own difficult circumstances.

I still live in my dream home in Rockville Centre, paying the mortgage without the help of a husband. I am a licensed real estate broker, massage therapist, and Reiki master. I am a good mother, a good friend, a good daughter, a good sister. I pay my bills and my taxes on time and live a modestly successful life. No longer would I accept a wad of cash from someone without asking him or her exactly how it was obtained. I suppose this makes me less trusting. I am single but I'm not hopeless; I'm sure that I will meet another best friend and lover whom I will marry someday. I know what it takes to make a relationship work now: open communication and trust as well as being brave enough to let your mate see your flaws and weaknesses, even as you strive to better yourself. After years of living on the surface of things, I now welcome the digging. The deeper I go in my search find answers, the more I know myself and the world around me. It feels good.

I believe in love. I believe in marriage and commitment. I believe in family. I believe in communicating. I believe in the truth. I believe in strength. Those things were not stolen from me, even though it may have felt that way at the time of Stephen's arrest.

For me, the journey continues. Blessings were in disguise as tragic events. Thanks to the love and support of so many people, I see now beyond the disguise and feel truly blessed.

Made in the USA
Middletown, DE
17 June 2023

32777141R00116